1975

This book may be kept

FOURTEEN DAYS

...day the book is kept overtime.

SAINT JOAN
OF THE STOCKYARDS

SAINT JOAN

of the

STOCKYARDS

A DRAMA BY BERTOLT BRECHT

translated by FRANK JONES
introduction by FREDERIC GRAB

 INDIANA UNIVERSITY PRESS
Bloomington & London

SECOND PRINTING 1971

Die heilige Johanna der Schlachthöfe by Bertolt Brecht
was originally published as the thirteenth experiment in
his *Versuche 5*, copyright 1932, by Gustav Kiepenheuer
Verlag A. G., Berlin.

Published in Canada by Fitzhenry & Whiteside Limited,
Don Mills, Ontario
Library of Congress catalog card number: 69-16006
Standard Book Number: 253-17671-9 [*Cl*]
253-20127-6 [*Pa*]
Manufactured in the United States of America

For Sumie

INTRODUCTION

Frederic Grab

May Day, 1929——in an unprecedented move, the police chief of Berlin had prohibited all workers' demonstrations, yet as the thirty-one-year-old Bertolt Brecht stood at the apartment window of his friend, the sociologist Fritz Sternberg, crowds kept gathering in front of the headquarters of the German Communist Party. A peaceful demonstration—until the police moved in. By the time they had cleared the streets, twenty people were dead. "I believe," wrote Sternberg, "this experience was not insignificant in driving [Brecht] ever more strongly to the Communists."[1] By the next year in Berlin one out of every three workers was jobless, and the violence became more common as the worldwide economic crisis deepened.

For Brecht, these rapidly changing social conditions presented aesthetic problems as well. In March 1929, he wrote:

> Simply to comprehend the new areas of subject matter imposes a new dramatic and theatrical form. Can we speak of money in the form of iambics? "The Mark, first quoted yesterday at 50 dollars, now beyond 100, soon may rise, etc."—how about that? Petroleum resists the five-act form; today's catastrophes do not progress in a straight line but in cyclical crises; the "heroes" change with the different phases, are interchangeable, etc.; the graph of people's actions is complicated by abortive actions; fate is no longer a single coherent power; rather there are fields of force which can be seen radiating in opposite directions; the power groups themselves comprise movements not only against one another but within themselves, etc., etc.[2]

What form should the drama now take, and what was the real nature of the reality which it should represent? Where and how, in brief, should the dramatist begin his analysis of society? In 1939 Brecht criticized the point of view of his early plays as being too immersed in process:

> My political knowledge in those days [presumably up to 1926] was disgracefully slight, but I was aware of huge inconsistencies in people's social life, and I didn't think it my task formally to iron out all the discordances and interferences of which I was strongly conscious. I caught them up in the incidents of my plays and in the verses of my poems; and did so long before I had recognized their real character and causes.[3]

Or, as he phrased it one year before his death, "It is scarcely possible to conceive of the laws of motion if one looks at them from a tennis ball's point of view."[4]

As for society, Brecht came to believe that its laws of motion could be understood only through a knowledge of Marx. In a short autobiographical piece written in the 1930's, Brecht looked back on his earlier career, in which he felt he had been unable initially to transcend a "rather nihilistic criticism of bourgeois society." Neither the films of Eisenstein nor the early productions of Erwin Piscator stimulated him to study Marx. Then, almost by accident, he decided to use the grain market of Chicago as background for his next play. But during his research he discovered that neither businessmen nor prominent writers on economics could adequately explain to him the events transpiring on the market. Gradually, Brecht came to the conclusion that these events were incomprehensible and irrational. "The drama I had planned," he concludes, "was never written; instead I began [in 1926] to read Marx and then for the first time I really *read* Marx. Then for the first time my own scattered practical experiences and impressions truly became alive and coherent."[5]

By 1926, then, Brecht had found a structure by which to analyze society—and a mode of thought by which he could construct drama as well. Although the play to which he here refers, *Joe Fleischhacker*, was never finished, nevertheless out of the readings he did for it came the awareness that, as he put it in 1927, "the works now being written are coming more and more to lead towards that great epic theater which corresponds to the sociological situation. . . ."[6] With the writing of *Saint Joan of the Stockyards* (1929–30), Brecht for the first time turned that hope into reality.

The idea for a play set in the Chicago stockyards may, in fact, have been in Brecht's mind as early as 1920. In an Augsburg theater review of that year, he speaks of his love for Schiller's *Don Carlos*, but goes on to add: "These days I've been reading in [Upton] Sinclair's *The Jungle* the history of a worker who starved to death in the stockyards of Chicago. It deals with plain hunger, cold, and sickness, which do a man in as surely as if they came from God. This man once has a small vision of freedom, but then is beaten down with billy clubs. I know his freedom has nothing at all to do with Carlos'—but I can no longer take Carlos' servitude seriously."[7] Here already is the antithesis between the idealism of German classical drama and the stark realities of life in the big city which form a basic structural element of *Saint Joan of the Stockyards. The Jungle*: the story of Lithuanian immigrants adrift in the city of Chicago, working in the stockyards where men were known to have slipped once and emerged from the plant in lard cans, and whose "laws and ways [were] no more than the universe to be questioned or understood."[8] But Brecht—like his heroine Joan—"wanted to know," and so in 1926, about the time in which he first came into contact with his Marxist "teacher," the philosopher Karl Korsch (who was himself expelled from the German Communist Party in 1926 for his heretical views), Brecht began to read Marx. In addition, as his life long friend and co-worker Elisabeth Hauptmann writes, he planned a series of plays on the general theme, "Entry of mankind into the big cities." Brecht himself had moved to

Berlin in 1924, and from 1925 to 1930 he worked on such projects as the above-mentioned story of the wheat king Joe Fleischhacker and the Mitchell family "from the Savannah"; *Dan Drew* (from Bouck White's *The Book of Daniel Drew; A Glimpse of the Fisk–Gould–Tweed Regime from the Inside*); *Aus Nichts Wird Nichts* (*Nothing Comes of Nothing*); and *The Downfall of the Egoist Johann Fatzer*. The most important of these fragments, *Der Brotladen* (*The Bread Shop*; recently arranged and performed by the Berliner Ensemble), tells of the good-hearted newspaper boy Washington Meyer who, caught up in the Berlin unemployment crisis of 1929–30, quarrels with the bakery capitalist Meininger, and meets a violent death when the latter calls in the police. "What use is goodness," asked Brecht in the poem "Was Nützt die Güte," written in exile, "When the good are immediately slain, or those are slain / To whom they are good?" The problematic nature of goodness in a corrupt society, in fact, would be a factor in many plays from this time on: one thinks of Kattrin, Simone Machard, Grusha, Shen Te—and Joan Dark.

During the economic crisis of the late 1920's, one group tried to combine goodness with practicality, doling out soup, music, and Christian love in an attempt "to set Him upright in a crumbling world": the Salvation Army, with a record of over sixty years' service to mankind. Brecht first became interested in this organization in 1928, and, with Elisabeth Hauptmann, soon thereafter walked the streets of Berlin visiting their soup kitchens and talking with the souls they tried to save. Plainly Brecht, like Joan, saw their charity as a valid attempt to alleviate the misery of the poor by supplying their physical needs in an environment which at least admitted the possibility of communal relationships. But their attempt to stand "above the battle" really means, as Snyder says, that they stand on the packers' side of the barricades: the "warring fronts" can hardly be united by good intentions alone. Joan ultimately realizes that social reformers can easily be manipulated by the ruling class:

> Like an answer to their prayers I came to the oppressors!
> Oh, goodness without results! Unnoticed attitude!
> I have altered nothing.

Brecht expressed the same point in his poem "Das
Nachtlager" ("The Place to Sleep"), written shortly after
Saint Joan of the Stockyards. It tells of a man who stood
in winter on a New York corner, offering a few homeless
wretches a place to spend the night. Brecht concludes:

> A few people have a place to sleep
> For one night the wind is kept from them
> The snow, bound for them, falls on the street
> But the world is not thereby changed
> Relationships between men do not thereby improve
> The age of exploitation is not thereby shortened.

Although there are some who would offer shelter to those
who are cold, is such action alone sufficient? What
constitutes, in brief, a dialectical view of goodness?

   The first play in which Brecht considered this problem in
relation to the Salvation Army and the capitalist system was
Happy End. Produced in September 1929, with songs by
Brecht, dialogue by Hauptmann (presumably in at least
partial collaboration with Brecht), and music by Kurt Weill,
this play with music tells of the attempts of Salvation Army
lieutenant Lilian Holiday to convert gangster chief Bill
Cracker, attempts which culminate in their marriage and the
incorporation of the gang into the Salvation Army. Despite
the presence in the cast of Carola Neher (for whom Brecht
also wrote the title role of *Saint Joan of the Stockyards*),
and with Peter Lorre as the Japanese pickpocket Dr.
Nakamura, the critics—doubtless expecting another
Threepenny Opera—condemned the work vigorously. Brecht
and Hauptmann decided on a revision, but this was never
made. Instead Brecht brought together motifs from it and
from all the fragments of the 1925–30 period, applied to
them his recently acquired knowledge of Marxism and his

rapidly developing theories of epic theater, and composed
Saint Joan of the Stockyards.

The form of this parable of religion and capitalism is that
of a Shakespearean history play. The verse includes
borrowings from Schiller's *The Maid of Orleans* (a blank
verse history play, in which Joan dies on the battlefield, with
the flag of France in her hand), the final scene of Goethe's
Faust II (Joan's canonization using several of the meters of
Faust's salvation), and even Hölderlin (in some of the free
verse passages). The content derives from Upton Sinclair,
Lincoln Steffens, and G. B. Shaw (*Major Barbara* more than
Saint Joan), among others. And the result: Brechtian epic—
or better, dialectical—theater. The parodistic borrowings,
moreover, exist not for parody alone, but to remind us of the
gap between concept and reality. The blank verse form,
used by the heroes of classical German drama, serves on
the one hand to disguise the crass business dealings of
Mauler and his associates (the ideological mask falling at
times as the tycoons lapse into prose), but at the same time
Brecht expects the audience to realize that the purpose of
the "parody" is both in its statement of a relationship and
in its creation of a "distancing (or alienation) effect" by
which that relationship can be judged. In other words, the
basis of the stylistic dialectic lies in the relationship
between the actions of the meat kings and their own
verbalized representations of those actions. Or as Roland
Barthes puts it, "Distancing [the French for *Verfremdung* is
distanciation] is not a form . . . it is the relationship of a
form and a content."[9] This is not to say, of course, that
Mauler is not sincere in his outpourings of iambic
pentameter; even his love of animals is a sincerely felt
ideological justification for his business dealings. The point,
however, is to unmask ideology (both Mauler's and Joan's),
and this Brecht does by localizing his action in the gap
between classical form and capitalist content.

In his attempt to answer the question, Is *Saint Joan of*

the Stockyards a "realistic work"? Brecht wrote: "The juxtaposition of the specific way the characters act with their mode of expression . . . may be bewildering, but in this way certain methods of representation are destroyed, by the demonstration of their social function—and that's realism!" And later:

> *Saint Joan of the Stockyards* is a non-Aristotelian drama. This type of drama demands a particular kind of attitude on the part of the spectator. He must be able to follow events on the stage from a specific, learnable point of view, and to comprehend them in their total context and development—and this with a view towards a fundamental revision of his own conduct. He must not spontaneously identify with certain characters, and then simply participate in their experience. He must not, in other words, proceed from his own intuition into their "Being," but should rather plot out the dynamics of their relationships on the basis of the characters' speeches and actions.[10]

Brecht, that is, is not interested solely in the "Being" of his characters, although in Mauler he created one of his greatest individuals. More important are the relationships prevailing between the characters, and the social laws which govern those relationships—laws which Joan (and, with less drastic results, Brecht himself) came to realize only after hard experience.[11] Her lonely awareness (reflected perhaps by the fact that only she speaks free verse in the final scene) is drowned out by the relentless, Goethean tetrameters of the packers, while Mauler— Faustian Man, Brecht called him—attempts (in a parody of the end of *Faust II*) to reunite his two souls in the interest of greater capital accumulation. In seven days, he has re-created Chicago and, with the aid of the Black Straw Hats, has managed to draw a veil of ideology over prevailing economic contradictions. As for Joan, Sullivan Slift— Mephisto to Mauler's Faust—realizes that at the end she is well on her way to becoming a threat to the established order. At last, her goodness has been combined with knowledge, and so she must die, in order that the capitalist cycle may continue.

In *Die Dramaturgie Brechts*, Käthe Rülicke points out that the entire play is a demonstration of the workings of the cycles of capitalist production. Brecht had read in *Capital* Marx's theory of how "the life of modern industry becomes a series of periods of moderate activity, prosperity, overproduction, crisis, and stagnation" (vol. I, ch. 16, section 7). The structure of the play is determined by these stages (each new stage in the cycle being introduced by a letter from Mauler's friends in New York), with the canonization scene showing how the cycle renews itself as monopolies are formed. Thus the laws of human economics are not (as the Small Speculators maintain, and as Brecht himself had once thought) "ever inscrutable," nor do all the workers believe the Black Straw Hats when they claim "that unhappiness does fall like the rain, nobody knows where from, and that suffering is their fate and a reward for it awaits them." This position is similar to that which Brecht (in his 1931 notes on "Die dialektische Dramatik") called the style of naturalism, which sees "milieu as fate," "unchangeable and inescapable." This was the position which the immigrant family in *The Jungle*, also, initially maintained; but for the Marxist Brecht, this attitude could be easily explained:

> The social power, i.e., the multiplied productive force, which arises through the co-operation of different individuals as it is determined within the division of labour, appears to these individuals, since their co-operation is not voluntary but natural, not as their own united power but as an alien force existing outside them, of the origin and end of which they are ignorant, which they thus cannot control, which on the contrary passes through a peculiar series of phases and stages independent of the the will and the action of man, nay, even being the prime governor of these (Marx and Engels, *The German Ideology*, ed. Pascal [New York, 1947], p. 24).

But "the will and the action of man" can be liberated, as Joan ultimately realizes. Here Marx also points the way, but Joan's final realization—"Only force [*Gewalt*] helps where force rules, and / only men help where men are"—suggests Lenin as well. Plainly Lenin's work had a decisive effect on Brecht. Writings such as *State and Revolution*, in fact, were appearing in Germany in the early 1920's—formative years in Brecht's development. Here and elsewhere Lenin criticized those who would revise Marxist doctrine in the interest of presenting evolution as the sole means of transforming society, rather than revolution. Hanns Eisler, in fact, in a 1961 interview pointed out that *Saint Joan of the Stockyards* is really "a Leninist play" because of its stress on the necessity for force (or violence) as the only agent capable of bringing about social change.[12] In 1926 (two years after Lenin's death) Brecht wrote: "[The fact that the capitalist system is still possible] proves that nothing will happen by means of evolution other than what has already happened, and that the ruling class must be removed by force [*Gewalt*]." Marx stressed this point, too, but its immediacy in Germany was perhaps due more to the example and the writings of Lenin. Hanns Eisler, in any case, preferred to call Brecht a Leninist, rather than a Marxist. Brecht may have derived some of his notions on the relationship between religion and economics from Lenin as well, for Lenin believed that "the religious oppression of humanity is only a product or reflex aspect of the economic oppression in society. . . . In modern capitalist countries the basis of religion is primarily *social*. The roots of modern religion are deeply embedded in the social oppression of the working masses, and in their apparently complete helplessness before the blind forces of capitalism. . . ."[13]

Only revolution can remove those "blind forces," as Brecht demonstrates in *The Mother* (written 1930–31), his only full-length play with a wholly positive leading figure. *The Mother*, one could say, completes the process begun in *Saint Joan of the Stockyards*: finally a social totality is formed, whereas the characters in Brecht's earlier plays (and virtually all of the later ones as well) are condemned to partiality, condemned to live—like Joan Dark—in ignorance of the gap between ideology and social practice. For us as spectators, however, this gap can be bridged by the epic theatrical production—not because a Brecht play offers ultimate answers (none of them ever do), but because, as Louis Althusser puts it, the epic theater deals with "the process of becoming, the production of a new consciousness in the audience—incomplete like all consciousnesses yet propelled by its very incompleteness, that acquired distance, that inexhaustible work of criticism in action; the play is indeed the making of a new play-goer, an actor who begins when the play ends, who begins only to give it a conclusion in real life."[14] *Saint Joan of the Stockyards*, finally, remains open-ended, waiting for those who see and read it to effect that re-structuring of experience which would supply its only possible conclusion.

NOTES

1. *Der Dichter und die Ratio* (Göttingen, 1963), p. 25; unless otherwise indicated, all translations in this introduction are mine. The quotations from the play are from this translation of *Saint Joan of the Stockyards* by Frank Jones.

2. *Brecht on Theater*, trans. Willett (New York, 1964), p. 30.

3. *Brecht on Theater*, p. 116.

4. *Brecht on Theater*, p. 275.

5. *Schriften zur Politik und Gesellschaft* (Frankfurt, 1968), p. 46.

6. *Brecht on Theater*, p. 21.

7. Review of April 15, 1920; *Schriften zum Theater*, I (Frankfurt, 1965), pp. 15-16.

8. New York, 1950 (reprint of first edition, 1905), p. 41.

9. "Seven Photo Models of Mother Courage," *The Drama Review*, XII (Fall 1967), 45.

10. *Schriften zum Theater*, II (Frankfurt, 1963), pp. 141, 143.

11. In the mid-1930's Brecht wrote: "The epic theater is chiefly interested in the attitudes which people adopt towards one another,

wherever they are socio-historically significant (typical)" (*Brecht on Theater*, p. 86).

12. "Fünftes Gespräch," *Sinn und Form* (Sonderheft Hanns Eisler, 1964), 294. Eisler uses Brecht's word *Gewalt,* which may also be translated *violence.*

13. *Religion* (New York: International Publishers, n. d.), pp. 14, 19.

14. As quoted by Bernard Dort, "Epic Form in Brecht's Theater," trans. Ostergren, *Yale / Theatre*, 2 (Summer 1968), 32.

AUTHOR'S NOTE

The intent of the thirteenth experiment, *Saint Joan of the Stockyards*, is to show the present-day stage in the evolution of Faustian man. The piece originated in the play *Happy End* by Elisabeth Hauptmann. In addition, several classical models and stylistic elements were employed: the representation of certain events was given the form historically ordained for it. Thus, not only the events are exhibited, but also the manner of their literary-theatrical subjugation.

1932

TRANSLATOR'S NOTE

In London in 1937 I noticed in a German refugee
bookstore a gray-covered pamphlet which looked like a
government report. Despite its appearance I bought
Versuche 5, comprising *Die heilige Johanna der
Schlachthöfe,* and another item "belonging," said the
prefatory note, "to Experiment 2." Fascinated by the play,
I praised it in an article on Brecht which was published in
1940. James Laughlin read the article and asked me to
translate the play. I did so in 1941, and fifteen years later
the translation was published in *From the Modern Repertoire,
Series Three* (Bloomington: Indiana University Press), edited
by Eric Bentley.

Since then the version has been thrice revised, and now
it is in large part rewritten. Among other things, two of
the four media of the original work—blank verse and rhyming
verse—are more scrupulously followed than before, and a
feature of Brecht's punctuation is retained: no verse line
ends with a comma.

As usual, all the mistakes I found have been corrected.
Mauler, however, still says in Scene IX, speaking in Chicago:
"from here to Illinois." Brecht must have thought this
either factual or funny, for he never changed it.

The first full performance of the original play took
place at the Hamburg Schauspielhaus in 1959, and it entered
the repertory of the Berliner Ensemble in 1968. This translation has had one production in Scotland and four in the
United States, and parts of it have been presented by the
Canadian Broadcasting Corporation. So far Brecht's Joan has
not been seen in Chicago, except in book form.

1969

SAINT JOAN
OF THE STOCKYARDS

CHARACTERS

PIERPONT MAULER ⎤
CRIDLE ⎪
FREDDY GRAHAM ⎬ *meat packers*
M. L. LENNOX ⎪
MEYERS ⎦

SULLIVAN SLIFT, *Mauler's broker*

JOAN DARK ⎤
MARTHA ⎪
MAJOR PAULUS SNYDER ⎬ *Black Straw Hats*
JACKSON ⎦

MULBERRY, *a landlord*
GLOOMB, *a worker*
SMITH, *a foreman*
MRS. LUCKERNIDDLE, *a worker's widow*
MRS. SWINGURN, *a worker*
AN APPRENTICE
A WAITER
AN OLD MAN
A BROKER
TWO DETECTIVES
TWO WORKERS' LEADERS
TWO POLICEMEN

*Brokers, Wholesalers, Stockbreeders, Small Speculators, Workers,
Reporters, Newsboys, Bystanders, Voices, Musicians, Soldiers,
Poor People*

I

Chicago stockyards.

Mauler (*reading a letter*) "It is plain to us, dear Pierpont,
that for some little time the meat market has been
glutted. Moreover, tariff walls south of the border are
resisting all our attacks. Therefore, dear Pierpont, it
seems advisable to pull out of the meat business." I have
this tip today from my good friends in New York. Here
comes my partner. (*hides letter*)

Cridle My good friend Pierpont! Why so gloomy?

Mauler Remember, Cridle, how, some days ago
  on our walk through the stockyards in the evening
  we stopped beside our new packing machine.
  Remember, Cridle, the steer, fair-haired and big
  and dully gazing heavenward as he took
  the blow: I felt that it was meant for me.
  Oh, Cridle, oh!
  Our business is bloody!

Cridle So, the old weakness, Pierpont?
  Almost incredible: you, giant of packers
  king of the stockyards, quaking at the kill
  dying in pain, all for a fair-haired steer!
  Pray, not a word of this, except to me.

Mauler O loyal Cridle!
  I ought not to have visited the stockyards!
  Since entering this business, seven years
  ago, I had kept out of them. Cridle, I can't
  face it any more, I'm clearing out today.
  You take the bloody business, with my interest.

> I'll let you have it cheap, you above all
> for no one else is so involved in it.

Cridle How cheap?

Mauler Among old friends like you and me
> that's not a point to haggle over. Say
> ten million.

Cridle That wouldn't be expensive but for Lennox
> who fights with us for every can of meat
> fouls up the market with his cut-throat prices
> and will break us all if he does not go broke.
> Until he falls, and only you can fell him
> I won't accept your offer. That's how long
> you'll have to keep your scheming brain in action.

Mauler No, Cridle, that steer's moaning can
> no more be stilled within this breast. And so
> this Lennox must fall speedily, for I
> am ready to become a decent man
> and not a butcher. Cridle, I'll tell you now
> what you must do to make the fall of Lennox
> a fast one. Then you must
> relieve me of this business, which pains me.

Cridle If Lennox falls. (*They leave*)

II

THE COLLAPSE OF THE BIG PACKING PLANTS

Outside the Lennox plant.

The Workers We are seventy thousand workers in the
> Lennox plant and we
> can't live a day longer on these low wages.
> Yesterday our pay took another cut
> and today the notice is up again:
> Anyone not satisfied
> with our wages may leave.

        All right then, let's all go and
        shit on the pay that's poorer day by day. (*pause*)
        For a long time now this work has made us sick
        the factory our hell and nothing
        but cold Chicago's terrors could
        keep us here. But now
        by twelve hours' work a man can't even
        earn a stale loaf and
        the cheapest pair of pants. Now
        a man might just as well go off and
        croak right away. (*pause*)
        What do they take us for? Do they think
        we'll stand around like steers, ready
        for anything? Are we
        their clowns? We'd rather die!
        Let's go right now. (*pause*)
        It must be six by now!
        Open up, butchers, your steers are here! (*They
           knock*)
        Maybe we've been forgotten? (*laughter*)
        Open the gates! We
        want to get inside your
        dirty holes and dingy kitchens
        to cook stuffed meat
        for its well-heeled eaters. (*pause*)
        We demand at least
        our former wages, even though they were too
          low, at least
        a ten-hour day and at least—

A Man (*passing by*)   What are you waiting for? Don't you
          know
        that Lennox has shut down?

Newsboys (*running across stage*)   Meat king Lennox
  forced to shut down his plants! Seventy thousand workers
  without food or shelter! M. L. Lennox a victim of the
  fierce competitive struggle with Pierpont Mauler,
  well-known meat king and philanthropist.

Workers Horror!
Hell itself
shuts its gate in our faces.
We are doomed. Bloody Mauler grips
our exploiter by the throat and
we are the ones who choke!

P. MAULER

A street.

Newsboys Chicago Tribune, noon edition! P. Mauler,
meat king and philanthropist, will attend the opening of
the P. Mauler Hospitals, largest and costliest in the world!
(*P. MAULER passes, with TWO MEN*)

Bystander (*to another*) That's P. Mauler. Who are the
men with him?

The Other Detectives. They guard him so that nobody
will knock him down.

TO COMFORT THE DISTRESS OF
THE STOCKYARDS, THE BLACK
STRAW HATS DEPART FROM THEIR
MISSION HOUSE. JOAN'S FIRST
DESCENT INTO THE DEPTHS

Outside the Black Straw Hat Mission.

Joan (*at the head of a Black Straw Hat shock troop*)
In a gloomy time of bloody confusion
ordered disorder
planful wilfulness
dehumanized humanity
when disturbances are unending in our cities:
into such a world, a world like a slaughterhouse

summoned by rumored threats of violence
to stop the brute strength of the dim-sighted
   people
from smashing its own tools and
crushing its own bread-basket underfoot
we wish to bring back
God.
Of little fame these days
almost disreputable
not admitted now
among realities:
but, for the lowest, the one salvation!
Therefore we have decided
to beat the drum for Him
so that He may find a footing in the districts of
   misery
and His voice may resound in the stockyards.
(to the BLACK STRAW HATS) And this enterprise of
   ours is surely
the last of its kind. A last attempt
to set Him upright in a crumbling world,
   and that
by means of the lowest.
(They march on, drums beating)

FROM DAWN TO DUSK THE BLACK
STRAW HATS LABORED IN THE
STOCKYARDS, BUT WHEN EVENING
CAME THEY HAD ACCOMPLISHED
JUST ABOUT NOTHING

Outside the Lennox packinghouses.
A Worker   They say there's another spell of dirty dealing
in the meat market. Till it's over I guess we'll have to bide
our time and live on air.

Another Worker   Lights are on in the offices. They're counting up the profits. (*The BLACK STRAW HATS arrive. They put up a sign: Bed for a night, 20 cents. With coffee, 30 cents. Hot dogs, 15 cents*)

Black Straw Hats (*singing*)

      Attention, pay attention!
      We see a man to save!
      We hear his cry for help
      We see a woman wave.
      Halt the autos, stop the streetcars too!
      Take heart, all fainting folk, we're on our way to
         you!
      If you're going under
      set eyes on us, brother, before you say you're
         beat!
      We'll get you things to eat
      We don't have to be told
      that you're still out in the cold.
      Don't say that nothing helps, for times are
         changing
      Injustice in the world shall not abide
      if all the people join us as we march
      forget their cares and follow in our stride.
      We'll bring up tanks and artillery
      and call the airplanes out
      and battleships over the sea
      because your dish of soup, brother, is what it's
         all about.
      You folk that are poor
      are an army vast and grand
      so these days all the more
      we've got to lend you a hand!
      Shoulder arms! Forward march! Keep ranks
         straight and true!
      Take heart, all fainting folk, we're on our way to
         you!

(*As they sing the BLACK STRAW HATS have been handing out their leaflet, "The Battle Cry," spoons, and soup. The WORKERS say "Thank you" and listen to Joan's speech*)

Joan   We are the Soldiers of the Lord. On account of our hats we are also called the Black Straw Hats. We march with drums beating and flags flying wherever unrest prevails and acts of violence threaten, to remind men of the Lord whom they have all forgotten, and bring back their souls to Him. We take the name of soldiers because we are an army and, as we march, we must battle crime and misery, which are always trying to drag us down. (*She begins to ladle out soup*) That's right, just have some hot soup and things will look all different, but please give a little thought to Him who bestows it on you. And when you think that way you will see that this is the entire solution: Strive upward, not downward. Get in line for a good job up above, not here below. Try to be the first above, not the first below. Surely you realize now how much trust you can put in the fortunes of this world. None at all. Trouble comes like the rain, that nobody maketh, and yet it comes. Can you tell me where all your troubles come from?

An Eater   From Lennox and Company.

Joan   Maybe Mr. Lennox has more worries now than you. What have you got to lose? His losses amount to millions!

A Worker   There's mighty little fat afloat in this soup, but it contains plenty of wholesome water and there's no lack of warmth.

Another Worker   Shut up, feasters. Hear the heavenly text or they'll take your soup away.

Joan   Quiet! Dear friends, why do you suppose you're poor?

Worker   Come on, give us the story.

Joan   Not because you aren't blest with worldly goods— that's not for all of us—but because you have no sense of higher values. That's why you're poor. Those low pleasures you work so hard to get, a bite to eat, nice homes, the movies, are nothing but coarse sensual enjoyments, but God's word is a far finer, more intimate,

more exquisite pleasure, maybe you can't think of
anything sweeter than whipped cream, but God's word is
sweeter still, oh, how sweet is the word of God! It is like
milk and honey, and in it ye dwell as in a palace of gold
and alabaster. O ye of little faith, the birds under heaven
have no Help Wanted ads and the lilies of the field have
no jobs, and yet He feeds them, because they hymn His
praise. You all want to reach the top, but what kind of
top, and how are you going to get there? And so it's we
Black Straw Hats who ask you, very practically: What
does a man need to rise?

Worker A stiff collar.

Joan No, not a stiff collar. Maybe you need a stiff collar
to get ahead on earth, but in God's eyes you need much
more than that around you, an entirely different kind of
glory, but before Him you haven't even a rubber collar to
wear, because you've entirely neglected everything
within you. And how will you reach the top—whatever
in your blindness you call the top—by brute force? As if
force ever caused anything but destruction! You believe
that if you rear up on your hind legs there'll be paradise
on earth. But I say unto you: that way not paradise but
chaos is created.

Worker (*running up*)   There's a job to be had!
        It pays, and it's calling you over
        to Plant Number Five!
        Outside, it looks like a piss-house.
        Run!

(*THREE WORKERS leave full soup-plates and run off*)

Joan Hey, where are you off to? Talk about God and you
don't want to hear, eh?

A Black Straw Hat Girl The soup's all gone.

Workers The bit of soup is gone.
        Fatless it was and scant, but
        better than nothing. (*All turn away and get up*)

Joan Oh, keep your seats, no harm done, the grand soup
of heaven never runs out, you know.

Workers When will you finally
            open your roachy cellars
            you butchers of men? (*Groups form*)
A Man How can I pay for my little house now, the cute
               damp thing
            with twelve of us in it? Seventeen
            payments I've made and now the last is due.
            They'll throw us out on the street and never again
            will we see the trampled ground with the yellowish
               grass
            and never breathe again
            the familiar pestilent air.
Second Man (*inside a circle*) Here we stand with hands
               like shovels
            and necks like trucks, ready to sell
            hands and necks
            and nobody wants them.
Workers And our tool, a giant pile
            of steam-hammers and cranes
            locked in behind walls!
Joan What's up? Now that bunch is leaving too. Had
   enough, friends? Fine, I hope it does you good. Why did
   you listen this long?
A Worker For the soup.
Joan We must be going. Sing!
Black Straw Hats (*singing*) Go straight to the thick of the
               fight
            where there's the hardest work to do.
            Sing with all your might! It may still be night
            but already the morning is coming so bright!
            Soon the Lord Jesus will come to you too.
Voice (*from rear*) There's still some work at Mauler's!
   (*The WORKERS, except a FEW WOMEN, leave*)
Joan (*gloomily*) Pack up the instruments. Did you see how
   they rushed off as soon as the soup was gone?
            This attains no greater height
            than the rim of a dish. It believes

in nothing that it cannot
hold in its hand—if it believes in hands.
Living unsurely from minute to minute
they can no longer lift themselves
from the lowest ground. Only
hunger is level with them. They
are moved by no song, no word
reaches them in those depths.
(*to the BYSTANDERS*)   We Black Straw Hats feel as
though we were expected to satisfy a starving continent
with our spoons.
(*The WORKERS return. Shouting in the distance*)

Workers (*front*)   Who's yelling like that? A huge stream of
people from over by the packinghouses!

Voice (*rear*)   Mauler and Cridle are shutting down too!
There's a lockout at the Mauler plant!

Returning Workers   Running for jobs, we met halfway
a stream of desperate men
who had lost their jobs and
asked us for jobs.

Workers (*front*)   Horror! That way, too, a line of men!
You can't see the end of it! And Mauler
has shut down too! What will become of us?

Black Straw Hats (*to JOAN*)   Come on. We're chilled to the
bone, and wet, and we've got to eat.

Joan   Whose fault is all this? That's what I want to know.

Black Straw Hats   Stop! Don't get mixed up in that! They're
sure
to give you an earful. There's nothing in their
minds
but what is vile. They're idlers!
Gluttonous slackers, from birth onward
empty of high ideals!

Joan   No, I want to know. (*to the WORKERS*)   Tell me,
now. Why are you running around without any work?

Workers   Bloody Mauler is locked in battle
with grasping Lennox and so we go hungry.

Joan   Where does Mauler live?

Workers   Over there where livestock is bought and sold
                in a big building, the Livestock Exchange.
Joan   There I shall go, for
                I must know this.
Martha   Don't meddle in that! One who asks many
                    questions
                gets many answers.
Joan   No, I intend to see this Mauler, who brings on
                such wretchedness.
Black Straw Hats   Then, Joan, your coming fate looks grim
                    to us.
                Keep out of earthly fights!
                The meddler in a fight becomes its victim!
                His purity swiftly perishes. Soon
                his bit of warmth perishes in the cold
                that rules over all. Goodness abandons him
                who flees the sheltering hearth.
                Groping down from step to step
                to find the answer that never will be yours
                you will disappear in dirt!
                Nothing but dirt is stuffed into the mouths
                of those who ask without caution.
Joan   I want to know.
    (*The BLACK STRAW HATS, except JOAN and MARTHA,*
    leave)

III

PIERPONT MAULER FEELS THE BREATH
OF ANOTHER WORLD

Outside the Livestock Exchange. Lower level: JOAN and
MARTHA, waiting. Upper level: the meat packers LENNOX
and GRAHAM, talking. LENNOX is deathly pale.

Graham   So, my good Lennox, you have felt the fist
of brutal Mauler. There's no hindering
this monster in his climb: nature to him
is merchandise, even the air's for sale.
What's in our stomachs he resells to us.
He gets rent out of caved-in houses, money
from rotten meat; stone him, he's sure to change
the stones to money; he's so wild for money
so natural in this unnaturalness
that even he cannot deny its power.
He's soft himself, you know, does not love money
cannot bear misery, cannot sleep at night.
Therefore you must approach him and say in a
  choking voice:
"Mauler, look at me and take your hand
off my throat. Think of your old age."
That's sure to frighten him. Perhaps he'll cry . . .

Joan (*to MARTHA*)   Only you, Martha, have followed me
this far. All the others
left me with warnings on their lips
as if I were going to extremes. Strange warning.
I thank you, Martha.

Martha   I also warned you, Joan.

Joan   And followed me.

Martha   But will you really recognize him, Joan?

Joan   I'll know him!

Cridle (*coming out on upper level*)
Well, Lennox, no more undercutting now.
You're finished now and I'll close up and wait
for the market to recover. I'll clean my yards
and give the knives a good oiling and order some
of those new packing machines by which a man
can save a pretty sum in labor costs.

Graham   Damnable times!
Waste lies the market, stuffed with merchandise.
Trade, that was once so flourishing, lies fallow.
Scuffling over a market that's long been glutted

> you wrecked your own prices by undercutting one
>> another: so
> do buffaloes, fighting for grass, trample to
>> shreds the grass they fight for.

(MAULER comes out with his broker, SLIFT, in a crowd of MEAT PACKERS. TWO DETECTIVES follow him)

The Meat Packers Who'll stick it out? That's the question now!

Mauler Lennox is felled. *(to LENNOX)* Admit it, you are
> finished.
> I now demand, Cridle, that you take over
> the packing plant as stated in our contract
> presuming Lennox finished.

Cridle Agreed: Lennox is finished. But also finished
> are good times on the market. Therefore, Mauler
> you must come down from ten million for your
>> shares!

Mauler What? The price stands
> here in the contract! Here, Lennox, see if this
> isn't a contract, with the price right on it!

Cridle Yes, but a contract made in better times!
> What can I do with a slaughterhouse alone
> when nobody will buy a can of meat?
> Now I know why you couldn't bear to watch
> more bullocks die: it was because their meat
> cannot be sold!

Mauler No, it's my heart
> that swells, affected by the creature's bellow!

Cridle O mighty Mauler, now I grasp the greatness
> in all you do. Ah, even your heart
> sees far ahead!

Lennox Mauler, I'd like to talk . . . once more . . .

Graham Aim for his heart, Lennox! Aim for his heart!
> It's a sensitive dust-hole!

(He hits MAULER in the pit of the stomach)

Mauler Ouch!

Graham You see, he has a heart!

Mauler Well, Freddy, now I'll fix it up with Cridle
so he can't buy a single can from you
because you punched me.

Graham You can't do that, Pierpy. That's mixing
private concerns with business.

Cridle O.K. with me, Pierpy. Just as you like.

Graham I have two thousand workers, Mauler!

Cridle Send 'em to the movies! Now, look, Pierpy, our
agreement isn't valid. (*He calculates in a notebook*)
When we settled the terms of your withdrawal, the shares,
of which you hold a third, as I do, stood at 390. You gave
them to me for 320, which was cheap. Today it's
expensive, because now they're down to 100. With the
market glutted the way it is, if I'm to pay your price I'll
have to throw the shares onto the market. If I do that
they'll drop to 70, and what can I use to pay you then?
Then I'll be finished.

Mauler If that's your word for me, Cridle, I surely must
get my money out of you right away
before you're finished.
I tell you, Cridle, I'm so scared
I'm coming out in sweat, the most I can let you
have is six days. What am I saying? Five days
if that's the way things are with you.

Lennox Mauler, look at me.

Mauler Lennox, you tell me if the contract says anything
about bad times.

Lennox No. (*He leaves*)

Mauler Some worry seems to be oppressing him
and I, wrapped up in deals (would I were not!)
did not perceive it! Oh, this beastly business!
Cridle, it sickens me. (*CRIDLE leaves*)
(*Meanwhile JOAN has summoned one of the DETECTIVES
and told him something*)

Detective Mr. Mauler, some people over there would like
to talk to you.

Mauler A ragged bunch, eh? With a look of envy, eh?

and violent, no doubt? I
can't see anyone.

Detective They're a pair from the Black Straw Hat
organization.

Mauler What kind of an organization is that?

Detective There are many of them and they have a wide
network and are respected among the lower classes,
where they are called the Soldiers of the Lord.

Mauler I've heard of them. Strange name:
the Lord's Soldiers . . . but
what do they want of me?

Detective They say they have something to discuss with
you.
(*During this the Exchange uproar has resumed:
Steers 43, Hogs 55, Heifers 59, etc.*)

Mauler All right, tell them I will see them.
But tell them this too: they may say nothing that I
don't talk about first. Nor must they burst into tears
or songs, least of all sentimental ones.
And tell them it would be most useful to them
if I should get the impression that they are
well-meaning persons with nothing to their discredit
who want of me nothing that I do not have.
Another thing: don't tell them I am Mauler.

Detective (*going over to JOAN*) He'll talk to you, but
you must ask no questions, only answer
the ones he puts to you.

Joan (*walking up to MAULER*) You are Mauler!

Mauler No, I'm not. (*pointing to SLIFT*) That's him.

Joan (*pointing at MAULER*) You are Mauler.

Mauler No, he is.

Joan You are.

Mauler How do you know me?

Joan Because you have the bloodiest face. (*SLIFT laughs*)

Mauler You laugh, Slift?
(*Meanwhile GRAHAM has run off*)

Mauler (*to JOAN*)   How much money do you people earn
          per day?

Joan   Twenty cents, but food and clothing are supplied.

Mauler   Thin clothes, Slift, and thin soup too, I guess.
          Yes, those clothes are probably thin and the soup
             not rich.

Joan   Mauler, why are you locking the workers out?

Mauler (*to SLIFT*)   The fact that they work without pay
          is remarkable, isn't it? I never heard
          of anything like that, a person working
          for nothing and none the worse. And in their eyes
          I see no fear
          of misery or Skid Row.

    (*to JOAN*)   Strange people, you Black Straw Hats.
          I won't ask what you want of me exactly.
          I know they call me—what a bunch of fools!—
          Mauler the Bloody, saying it was I
          that ruined Lennox or caused inconvenience
          for Cridle, who is, between ourselves, a man
          of little worth. To you I may declare:
          These are commercial matters which you won't
          find interesting. But there's something else on
             which
          I'd like to have your views. I'm thinking of
             dropping
          this bloody trade as soon as possible.
          Recently—this will interest you—I saw
          a steer die and it shook me so
          that I'm giving it all up, and have even sold my
             interest
          in the factory, twelve million dollars' worth. I gave
             it to that man
          for ten. Don't you feel
          that this is right and to your liking?

Slift   He saw the steer die and decided
          to slaughter rich man Cridle

> instead of the poor steer.
> Was that right? *(THE PACKERS laugh)*

Mauler Go on, laugh. It's no skin off my back. Some day
> I'll see you cry.

Joan Mr. Mauler, why have you shut down the
> slaughterhouses?
> I have to know.

Mauler Was it not an astounding deed to take my hand
> out of a mighty concern, simply because it's
> bloody?
> Say that it's right and to your liking.
> No, don't tell me, I know, I admit, there are
> some who did poorly out of it, they lost
> their jobs, I know. Too bad, it couldn't be helped.
> A mean lot anyway, a tough crew, better not go
> near them, but tell me:
> my act in withdrawing from the business
> is surely right?

Joan I don't know if your question is serious.

Mauler That's because my damned voice is used to faking
> and so I know: you
> don't like me. Not a word.

(to the others) I feel as if a breath from another world
> were wafting toward me.

*(He takes all the money from everybody and gives it to
JOAN)*

> Out with your money, cattle-butchers, out with it
> now!

(He takes it from their pockets, gives it to JOAN)

> Take it, girl, to give to the poor!
> But rest assured that I feel no sort of obligation
> and sleep extremely well. Why am I helping here?
> Maybe
> just because I like your face, because it's so naive,
> although
> you've lived for twenty years.

Martha (*to JOAN*)   I don't believe that he's sincere in this.
Forgive me, Joan, for going away now too:
it looks to me as if you also
should leave all this alone. (*She leaves*)

Joan   Mr. Mauler, you know this is only a drop in the
bucket. Can't you give them real help?

Mauler   Spread the word that I warmly commend your
activity
and wish there were more like you. But
you musn't take this thing about the poor that way.
They're wicked people. Human beings don't touch
me:
they're not guiltless, and they're butchers too. But
let's drop all that.

Joan   Mr. Mauler, they're saying in the stockyards that their
misery is your fault.

Mauler   On oxen I have pity, man is wicked.
Mankind's not ripe for what you have in mind.
Before the world can change, humanity
must change its nature.
One moment, please.

(*in a low voice, to SLIFT*)
Give her more money away from here, when she's
alone.
Say it's for her poor, so she can take it
without blushing, but then see what she buys for
herself.
If that doesn't help, and I would like it not to
then take her with you
to the stockyards and show her
those poor of hers, how mean and beastly they are,
all treachery and cowardice
and how it's all their fault.
Maybe that will help.

(*to JOAN*)   This is Sullivan Slift, my broker. He's going to
show you something.

(*to SLIFT*)   I tell you, it's almost more than I can stand

　　　that there should be people like this girl, owning
　　　　　nothing
　　　but a black hat and twenty cents a day and
　　　　　fearless. (*He leaves*)
Slift (*to JOAN*)　I wouldn't care to know what you want to
　　　　　know
　　　but if you want to know it, come back tomorrow.
Joan (*watching MAULER go*)　That is no wicked man, he is
　　　　　the first
　　　to be scared from the thickets of vileness by our
　　　　　drums
　　　the first to hear the call.
Slift (*leaving*)　I advise you not to take up with those people
　　　　　down in the yards, they're a vile lot, frankly
　　　the scum of the earth.
Joan　I want to see it.

IV

THE BROKER SULLIVAN SLIFT SHOWS JOAN DARK THE WICKEDNESS OF THE POOR: JOAN'S SECOND DESCENT INTO THE DEPTHS

The stockyards district.
Slift　Now, Joan, I will show you
　　　　　the wickedness of those
　　　　　for whom you feel pity and
　　　　　that it is misplaced.
(*They are walking alongside a factory wall bearing the words "Mauler and Cridle, Meat Packers." The name Cridle has been crossed out with paint. TWO MEN come out by a little gate. SLIFT and JOAN hear their conversation*)

Foreman (*to a young APPRENTICE*) Four days ago a man
named Luckerniddle fell into our boiler, we couldn't stop
the machines soon enough so he got caught in the bacon-
maker, a dreadful thing to happen, this is his coat and
this is his cap, take them and get rid of them, all they do
is take up a hook in the cloakroom and make a bad
impression. It would be a good plan to burn them, right
now would be best. I'm entrusting the things to you
because I know you're a reliable man. I'd lose my job if
the stuff was found anywhere. Of course as soon as the
plant opens again you can have Luckerniddle's spot.

Apprentice You may rely on me, Mr. Smith (*The FOREMAN
goes back in through the gate*) Too bad about the man
that has to go out in the world as bacon, and really too
bad about his coat, it's still in good condition. Old Man
Bacon has his can to wear and he won't need this any
more, but I'd have plenty of use for it. Shit, I'll take it.
(*He puts it on and wraps his own coat and cap in
newspaper*)

Joan (*swaying*) I feel sick.

Slift That's the world as it is. (*stopping the YOUNG MAN*)
Say, where did you get that coat and cap? Didn't they
belong to Luckerniddle, the man that had the accident?

Apprentice Please don't let it get around, sir. I'll take the
things off right away. I'm in bad shape these days. The
extra twenty cents you earn in the manure cellars led me
to work on the bone-grinder last year. There I got lung
trouble and a chronic eye inflammation. My efficiency has
gone down since then and I've only been taken on twice
since February.

Slift Keep the things on. And come to Canteen Seven
today at noon. You'll get a free lunch and a dollar there
if you tell Luckerniddle's wife where you got that cap and
coat.

Apprentice Isn't that pretty rough, sir?

Slift Well, if you don't need the money . . .

Apprentice You may rely on me, sir. (*JOAN and SLIFT
walk on*)

Mrs. Luckerniddle (*sits complaining in front of the factory gate*)

> You in there, what are you doing with my husband?
> Four days ago he went to work, he said:
> Warm up the soup for me tonight! And still
> he isn't back! What have you done with him
> you butchers! Four days now I've been standing
>   here
> in the cold, nights too, waiting, but nobody tells me
> anything, and my husband doesn't come out! But
>   I tell
> you, I'm going to stand right here until I get
> to see him and you'll be sorry if you've done him
>   any harm!

Slift (*walking up to the WOMAN*)   Your husband is away, Mrs. Luckerniddle.

Mrs. Luckerniddle   Oh, don't give me that again.

Slift   I'll tell you something, Mrs. Luckerniddle, he's gone away and it's very embarrassing for the factory to have you sit around here talking foolishness. So we'll make you an offer which could not be required of us by law. If you drop your inquiries about your husband, you may eat lunch in our canteen every day for three weeks, free.

Mrs. Luckerniddle   I want to know what's happened to my husband.

Slift   We're telling you, he's gone to Frisco.

Mrs. Luckerniddle   He has not gone to Frisco. You got him into something and you're trying to cover it up.

Slift   If that's your opinion, Mrs. Luckerniddle, you can't accept any meals from the factory, but you'll have to bring suit against the factory. Well, think it over carefully. You can see me in the canteen tomorrow if you want. (*He moves back to JOAN*)

Mrs. Luckerniddle   I must have my husband back. I have no one but him to support me.

Joan   She will never come.

> Twenty lunches may mean a lot

48

to a hungry man, but
there is more for him.

(*JOAN and SLIFT walk on. They stop in front of a factory canteen and see TWO MEN looking in at a window*)

Gloomb There sits the supervisor whose fault it is that I caught my hand in the tin-slicer—stuffing his belly. We've got to make sure this is the last time the bastard stuffs himself at our expense. Better give me your club, mine might break in two.

Slift Stay here. I'm going to talk to him. And if he comes up to you, tell him you're looking for work. Then you'll see what kind of people these are. (*He goes up to GLOOMB*) Before you get carried away into doing something—that's how it looks to me—I'd like to make you a profitable proposition.

Gloomb I have no time right now, sir.

Slift Too bad. There would have been something in it for you.

Gloomb Make it short. We can't afford to let the bastard go. He's got to get his pay today for the inhuman system he cracks the whip for.

Slift May I suggest a way you could help yourself? I'm an inspector in the factory. Much inconvenience has been caused by the vacancy at your machine. Most people think the spot's too dangerous, just because of the fuss you've been making about your fingers. It would be great if we could fill that position. For instance, if you were to bring somebody along for it, we'd be ready at once to take you on again. In fact, we could get you an easier and better paying job than any you've had up to now. Maybe even the foreman's job. You look smart to me. And that fellow in there happens to have got himself disliked lately. You understand. You'd be in charge of tempo, of course, but first and foremost, as I've said, you must find someone for the spot at the tin-slicer, which, I admit, is none too safe. There's a girl over there, for instance, looking for work.

Gloomb Can a man rely on what you say?

Slift   Yes.

Gloomb   That one? She looks weak to me. It's no job for
people who tire quickly. *(to the other)* I've thought it over,
we'll do it tomorrow night. Night's a better time for games
like that. See you later. *(goes over to JOAN)* Looking
for a job?

Joan   Yes.

Gloomb   Eyesight good?

Joan   No. Last year I worked at the bone-grinder in the
manure cellars. There I got lung trouble and a chronic
eye inflammation. My efficiency has gone way down since
then. I've been out of a job since February. Is this a good
post?

Gloomb   A fine post. Work that even weaker people like
yourself can do.

Joan   Are you sure there's nothing else open? I've been
told that work on that machine is dangerous for people
who tire quickly. Their hands get unsteady and they grab
at the blades.

Gloomb   None of that is true. You'll be amazed to find how
pleasant the work is. You'll scratch your head and wonder
how people can tell such silly stories about that machine.
(SLIFT laughs and pulls JOAN away)

Joan   Now I'm almost afraid to go on. What will I see next?
*(They enter the canteen and see MRS. LUCKERNIDDLE,
talking to the WAITER)*

Mrs. Luckerniddle *(calculating)*   Twenty lunches . . . then
I could . . . then I'd go and then I'd have . . . *(She sits
down at a table)*

Waiter   If you're not eating you'll have to leave.

Mrs. Luckerniddle   I'm waiting for someone who was going
to come in today or tomorrow. What's for lunch today?

Waiter   Peas.

Joan   There she sits.
>   I thought she was quite firm and feared all the
>   same

that she would come tomorrow and now she has
run faster than we
and has arrived and is awaiting us.

Slift Go take her the food yourself. Maybe she'll think it over.

(*JOAN fetches the food and brings it to MRS. LUCKERNIDDLE*)

Joan So you've come today.

Mrs. Luckerniddle You see, I've had nothing to eat for two days.

Joan But you didn't know we would come today?

Mrs. Luckerniddle That's right.

Joan On the way over I heard that your husband had a mishap in the factory, for which the factory is to blame.

Mrs. Luckerniddle Oh, so you've reconsidered your offer? I don't get my twenty meals?

Joan But you got along well with your husband, from what I hear. People told me he's all you have.

Mrs. Luckerniddle Well, I've had nothing to eat for two days.

Joan Won't you wait till tomorrow? If you give up your husband, there'll be no one to ask about him. (*MRS. LUCKERNIDDLE is silent*) Don't take it.

(*MRS. LUCKERNIDDLE snatches the food from her hands and starts to eat greedily*)

Mrs. Luckerniddle He's gone to Frisco.

Joan And cellars and storehouses are full of meat
which can't be sold and is going rotten
because nobody takes it away.

(*The APPRENTICE with the coat and cap enters, rear*)

Apprentice Hello. Is this where I eat?

Slift Just take a seat beside the woman over there.
(*APPRENTICE sits down*) That's a good-looking cap you have. (*APPRENTICE hides cap*) Where did you get it?

Apprentice Bought it.

Slift Where did you buy it?

Apprentice Not in any store.

Slift   Then where did you get it?

Apprentice   I got it off a man that fell into a boiler.
(*MRS. LUCKERNIDDLE is nauseated. She gets up and goes out*)

Mrs. Luckerniddle (*on the way out, to the WAITER*)   Leave the plate where it is. I'll be back. I'll come every day at noon. Just ask that gentleman. (*She leaves*)

Slift   For three whole weeks she will come and feed, without looking up, like a beast. Now do you see, Joan, that their wickedness has no limits?

Joan   But how you rule
their wickedness! How you use it!
Don't you see that their wickedness hasn't a
    chance?
Certainly she would have liked
to be true to her husband as others are
and ask about the man who supported her
for a while longer, as a woman should.
But the price was too high: it came to twenty
    meals.
And would the young man on whom
any scoundrel can rely
have shown the coat to the dead man's wife
if things had been up to him?
He found the price too high
and why should the one-armed man have failed
to warn me? if the price
of so small a scruple were not so high for him?
Why did he sell his anger instead, which is
    righteous but too expensive?
If their wickedness has no limits, their poverty
has none either. Not the wickedness of the poor
have you shown me, but
the poverty of the poor.
Now that you've shown how wicked are the poor
I'll show you next the troubles at their door.
Brand of depravity, premature disgrace!
Be contradicted by their stricken face!

V

JOAN INTRODUCES THE POOR TO THE LIVESTOCK EXCHANGE

The Livestock Exchange.

The Packers We have canned meat for sale!
　　　　　Wholesalers, buy canned meat!
　　　　　Fresh, juicy canned meat!
　　　　　Mauler and Cridle's Bacon!
　　　　　Graham's Sirloins, soft as butter!
　　　　　Wilde's Kentucky Bargain Lard!

The Wholesalers And there was silence over the waters
　　　　　and
　　　　　a bust among the wholesalers!

Packers By means of mighty technical advances
　　　　　devotion of engineers and entrepreneurial vision
　　　　　we have managed to get the prices
　　　　　of Mauler and Cridle's Bacon
　　　　　Graham's Sirloins, soft as butter
　　　　　Wilde's Kentucky Bargain Lard
　　　　　reduced by one-third!
　　　　　Wholesalers, buy canned meat!
　　　　　Seize your opportunity!

Wholesalers And there was silence on the mountaintops
　　　　　and hotel kitchens veiled their heads
　　　　　and stores turned away in horror
　　　　　and middlemen went pale!
　　　　　We wholesalers throw up if
　　　　　we see a can of meat. The country's stomach
　　　　　has gobbled too much meat from cans
　　　　　and it's fighting back.

Slift What do you hear from your friends in New York?

Mauler   Theories. If things were up to them
            the whole meat ring would have to land in the
               muck
            and stay there for weeks till it nearly choked
            and I'd have all that meat around my neck!
            Madness!
Slift   Wouldn't it be funny if those fellows in New York
            really got tariffs lowered, opened things up below
               the border
            and started a sort of boom and we
            turned out to miss the bus?
Mauler   What if we did? Would you be callous enough
            to slice your meat from misery like that
            of these men here, watching like hawks
            for any kind of action? I couldn't be so callous.
Wholesalers   Here we stand, wholesalers with mountains
               of cans
            and cellars full of frozen cattle
            wanting to sell the cattle in cans
            and nobody demands it!
            And our customers, the kitchens and stores
            are stuffed to the ceiling with frozen meat
            and bellowing for buyers and eaters!
            No more buying for us!
Packers   Here we stand, packers with slaughterhouse and
               packroom
            yards full of cattle, day and night the machines
            run on under steam, brine, tubs and boilers
            wanting to turn the lowing ravenous herds
            into canned meat and nobody wants canned meat.
            We're ruined!
The Stockbreeders   And what about us stockbreeders?
            Who'll buy livestock now? In our barns stand
            cattle and hogs eating expensive corn
            and they ride to town in trains and while they ride
            they eat and at the stations
            in rent-devouring boxcars they wait, forever eating.

Mauler And now the knives wave them away.
Death, giving livestock the cold shoulder
closes his shop.

Packers (*shouting at MAULER, who is reading the paper*)
Traitorous Mauler, nest-befouler!
Do you think we don't know who's selling livestock
here
—oh, so secretly—and knocking the bottom out of
prices?
You've been offering meat for days!

Mauler Insolent butchers, howl in your mothers' laps
because the hunted creature's outcry ceases!
Go home and say that one of all your number
could not hear oxen bellow any longer
and would rather hear your bellow than their
bellow!
I want my money and quiet for my conscience!

A Broker (*bellowing from Exchange entrance, rear*)
Terrific drop in Stock Exchange quotations!
Huge sales of stocks. Cridle, formerly Mauler
drag the whole meat ring's rates down with them
into the abyss.

(*An uproar starts among the PACKERS. They rush at
CRIDLE, who is deathly pale*)

Packers What's the meaning of this, Cridle? Give it to us
straight!
Dumping stocks, with the market the way it is?

Brokers At 115!

Packers Got crap in your head?
It's not just you you're ruining by this!
You shit! You criminal!

Cridle (*pointing at MAULER*) Tell it to him!

Graham (*standing in front of CRIDLE*)
Cridle's not doing it, there's someone else
fishing and we're supposed to be the fish!
Some people want to get at the meat ring now
and wipe it out! Mauler, defend yourself!

Packers (*to MAULER*)

>Mauler, it's rumored that you're squeezing your
>>money
>from Cridle, who's already on the brink, and Cridle
>says not a word and points at you.

Mauler If I leave my money in Cridle's hands for another
>>hour—
>a man who's told me himself that he's unsound—
>>which of you
>could respect my head for business after that?
>>And I want nothing
>so much as *your* respect.

Cridle (*to those surrounding him*)   Exactly four weeks ago
I made a contract with Mauler. He wanted to sell me his
shares, one-third of the total, for ten million dollars. From
that time on, as I've only learned today, he's been selling
huge amounts of livestock, cheap, and on the sly, making
a still worse mess of prices that are dropping as it is. He
could demand his money whenever he pleased. I intended
to pay him by unloading part of his shares on the market
—they were high then—and reinvesting part. Then the
bottom fell out, and today Mauler's shares are worth not
ten but three million, and the whole plant is only worth
ten, not thirty million. That ten million is exactly what I
owe Mauler, and that's what he wants overnight.

Packers If you're doing this, making it hard for Cridle
>whose affiliates we are not, then you know well
>that this concerns us too. You're stripping all
>business bare, the fault is yours alone
>that our cans of meat are now as cheap as dirt
>because you ruined Lennox with cheap cans!

Mauler You shouldn't have slaughtered all that livestock,
>>you
>raving butchers! Now I want my money
>if it makes beggars of you all, my money
>must return! I have other plans.

Stockbreeders Lennox down! And Cridle groggy! And Mauler
pulls all his money out!

The Small Speculators
To us, small speculators, oh, nobody
gives a thought. Those who cry out
as the colossus topples do not see
where it falls, whom it crushes. Mauler, our money!

Packers Eighty thousand cans at 50, and fast!

Wholesalers Never a one!

(*Pause, during which the BLACK STRAW HATS'
drumming and JOAN's voice are heard*)

Joan's Voice Pierpont Mauler! Where is Mauler?

Mauler What's that drumming? Who
calls my name?
Here, where every man
shows his bare chops besmeared with blood!

(*The BLACK STRAW HATS enter, singing their war chant*)

Black Straw Hats Attention, pay attention!
There is a man to save!
There is a cry for help
There is a woman's wave.
Halt the autos, stop the streetcars too!
Folk falling all around and not a look from you!
Have you totally lost your sight?
Salute your brother, then you'll see the light!
Get up from that big meal
Can you no longer feel
for the many out there in the night?
I hear you say: it will always be the same
the injustice of the world will still abide.
But we say unto you: you've got to march
forget your cares and follow in our stride
and bring up tanks and artillery
and call the airplanes out
and warships over the sea—
a dish of soup for the poor is what it's all about.

Everyone lend us a hand
and that must be today
for the army of the good
is not a vast array.
Shoulder arms! Forward march! Keep ranks
　　straight and true!
Folk falling all around and not a look from you!

(*The Exchange battle has continued during this, but
laughter, prompted by shouts, is spreading toward stage
front*)

Packers　Eighty thousand cans at half price, and fast!

Wholesalers　Never a one!

Packers　That fixes us, Mauler.

Joan　Where is Mauler?

Mauler　Don't go now, Slift! Graham, Meyers
　　stay there in front of me.
　　I don't want to be seen here.

Stockbreeders　Not a steer to be sold in Chicago any more
　　this day spells ruin for all of Illinois
　　with mounting prices you prodded us into raising
　　　livestock
　　here we stand with livestock
　　and nobody wants it.
　　Mauler, you hound, the disaster is your fault.

Mauler　No dealings now. Graham, my hat. I've got to go!
　　A hundred dollars for my hat.

Cridle　Damn you to hell. (*He leaves*)

Joan (*behind MAULER*)　You just stay there, Mr. Mauler,
and listen to what I have to tell you. It's something for you
all to hear. Quiet!

　　No, indeed, you don't like us Black Straw Hats to turn
up in the dark hidden places where you do your business!
I've heard how you carry on here, making meat more and
more expensive by your sharp practices and tricky deals.
But if you thought you could keep it hidden you're off
the track, now and on His Judgment Day, for then it will
be revealed, and how will you look when our Lord and

Savior has you come up in a row and asks with His big
eyes: Where are my cattle now? What have you done with
them? Did you make them available to the people at
prices they could afford? Then where have they ended
up? And while you stand there embarrassed, groping for
excuses, as you do in your papers, which don't always
print the truth either, the cattle will bellow at your backs
in all the barns where you stash them away to make their
prices go sky-high, and by their bellowing they will bear
witness against you before Almighty God! (*Laughter*)

Stockbreeders We stockbreeders see nothing funny in
        that!

        At the mercy of weather, summer and winter, we
        stand
        considerably nearer the God of old.

Joan Now for an example. If a man builds a dam against
the unreasonable water, and a thousand people help him
with the labor of their hands and he gets a million for it,
but the dam gives way as soon as the water rises and
everybody working on it and many more are drowned—
what sort of man would build a dam like that? You may
call him a business man or a rascal, as you please, but
we say unto you that he's a blockhead. And all you men
who make bread dear and life a hell for human beings,
so that they all turn devils, are just plain dumb: paltry,
wretched blockheads, nothing else!

Wholesalers (*yelling*) By your unscrupulous
        juggling with prices and filthy lust for profit
        you're ruining yourselves!
        Blockheads!

Packers (*retorting*) You're the blockheads!
        Nothing can be done about crises!
        Unshakable above us
        stands economic law, the not-to-be-known.
        Terrible is the cyclic recurrence
        of natural catastrophes!

Wholesalers Nothing to be done about the way you're
        strangling us?

Wickedness, that's what it is, calculated
wickedness!

Joan   Now why is this wickedness in the world? Well, how
could it be otherwise? Of course, if a man has to bash his
neighbor's head in for a bit of ham on his bread, so as
maybe to grab from him what are, after all, the necessities
of life, brother clashing with brother over elementary
needs, how can any feeling for higher things stay alive in
the human heart? You might consider helping your
neighbor simply as serving a customer. Then you'll
understand the New Testament in a flash, and see how
basically modern it is, even today. Service! Why, what is
service but loving your neighbor—rightly understood, that
is! My dear sirs, I keep hearing that the poor have not
enough morals, and it's true. Immorality breeds down
there in the slums, and revolution goes along with it.

I ask you: Where are their morals to come from, if
morals are all they have? Where can they get anything
without stealing it? My dear sirs, there is such a thing as
moral purchasing power. Raise that and you'll get
morality too. And by moral purchasing power I mean
something very simple and natural: money. Wages. And
that brings me back to the facts of the matter. If you go
on like this you'll end up eating your meat yourselves,
because the people out there lack purchasing power.

Stockbreeders (*reproachfully*)   Here we stand with
livestock
and nobody wants it.

Joan   But ye sit here high and mighty, thinking no one will
ever catch you at your tricks, and turning your backs on
all the misery out there in the world. Well, then, take a
look at them, the people whom you have brought to this
pass, and whom you refuse to recognize as your
brothers. Come forth, ye weary and heavy laden, into the
light of day. Be not ashamed.

(*JOAN shows the Exchange CROWD the POOR whom
she has brought along*)

Mauler (*shouts*)   Take them away. (*He faints*)

Voice (*rear*)   Pierpont Mauler has fainted.

The Poor   He's the one. It's all his fault!

(*The PACKERS attend to MAULER*)

Packers   Water for Pierpont Mauler!
          A doctor for Mauler!

Joan   Mauler, you showed me the wickedness
          of the poor, so I am showing you
          the poverty of the poor. Far from you and others
             like you
          and removed thereby from indispensable goods
          live the people out of sight, whom you
          hold down in poverty like this, so weakened and
             in such pressing
          dependence on unattainable food and warmth that
             they
          are likewise far removed from any claim
          to higher things than basest gluttony, beastliest
             habituation.

(*MAULER regains consciousness*)

Mauler   Are they still here? I beg you, put them out.

Packers   The Black Straw Hats? You want them sent away?

Mauler   No, those others, behind them.

Slift   He won't open his eyes until they've gone.

Graham   Can't bring yourself to look at them, eh? But it
             was you
          that brought them to this pass.
          You may shut your eyes but it'll be long
          before they go.

Mauler   I beg you, put them out! I'll buy!
          Listen, all of you: Pierpont Mauler's buying!
          To get these people work and get them out.
          All the canned meat you produce in eight weeks:
          I'll buy it.

Packers   He's bought! Mauler has bought!

Mauler   At today's price!

Graham (*holding him up*)   What about reserves?

Mauler (*lying on the floor*)　I'll buy 'em.

Graham　At 50?

Mauler　At 50!

Graham　He's bought! You heard it, he has bought!

Brokers (*shouting through megaphones, rear*)　Pierpont
　Mauler props up the meat market. He has contracted to
　take over at today's price of 50 the total reserves of the
　meat ring, plus two months' output, from today on, also
　at 50. The meat ring will deliver at least 400 tons of
　canned meat to Pierpont Mauler on November 15.

Mauler　But now, my friends, I beg you, carry me out.
　(*MAULER is carried out*)

Joan　That's fine, have yourself taken away!
　　　　　We work at our mission jobs like plow-horses.
　　　　　And this is the kind of thing you do up here!
　　　　　You had me told I shouldn't say a word, but
　　　　　who are you
　　　　　to try to muzzle the Lord in His goodness? You
　　　　　　shouldn't
　　　　　even muzzle the ox that's yoked to the thresher!
　　　　　And so I speak.
　(*to the POOR*)　You'll have work again on Monday.

Poor　We never saw people like that before. But better
　them than those two standing beside him. They look far
　worse than he does.

Joan　Now sing in farewell the song: Who shall ever lack
　for bread.

Black Straw Hats (*singing*)　Who shall ever lack for bread
　　　　　once his soul to the Lord is given?
　　　　　A man will never be in need
　　　　　if he stays within God's grace.
　　　　　For how can snow fall in that haven?
　　　　　And how can hunger find that place?

Wholesalers　The fellow's sick in the head. The country's
　　　　　stomach
　　　　　has gobbled too much meat from cans and it's
　　　　　fighting back.

And he has meat put into cans
that nobody will buy. Strike out his name.

Stockbreeders Come on, up with those prices, you rotten
butchers!

Until you double what you pay for livestock
not an ounce will be delivered. Now you need it.

Packers Keep your crap! You won't get us to buy it.
The contract which you saw agreed on here
is a scrap of paper. The man who made it was
not in his right mind. He couldn't raise
a cent from Frisco to New York
for a deal like that. (*They leave*)

Joan Well, anyone who really cares for God's word and
what He says and not just what the ticker tape says, and
there must be some people here that are respectable and
conduct their business in a God-fearing way, we have
nothing against that—he's welcome to visit our Divine
Services on Lincoln Street, Sunday at two, music after
three, admission free.

Slift (*to the STOCKBREEDERS*) What Pierpont Mauler
promises, he does.

Now we may watch the market getting well!
Givers and takers of our bread, breathe free!
At last we've overcome the evil spell
that threatened confidence and harmony!
Ye that take work, ye that have work to give
are opening the doors by which we live!
Victory over folly came about
by wisdom's counsel, wisely carried out.
The gates swing wide! The smokestacks belch
again!
We're back at work, the common need of men.

Stockbreeders (*placing JOAN up on the stairs*)

Your speech and presence impressed us
stockbreeders
very much and many a man here
was shaken to the roots, for we
have terrible sufferings too.

Joan You know, I have my eye
on Mauler, he's awake, and as for you
if there's anything you need in this emergency
come with me, so he'll put you back on your feet
because from now on he won't be left in peace
till everyone is helped.
He is able to help and so
let's find him.

(*JOAN and the BLACK STRAW HATS leave, followed by
the STOCKBREEDERS*)

VI

THE CRICKET CAUGHT

*City. The broker Sullivan Slift's house, a small one with
two entrances.*

Mauler (*inside the house, talking to SLIFT*) Barricade the
door, turn on all the lights, then take a good look at my
face, Slift, to see if everyone can tell.

Slift Tell what?

Mauler What I do for a living.

Slift Butchery? Mauler, why did you fall down when she
spoke?

Mauler What was she talking about? I didn't
hear, because at her back
there stood such people with such ghastly faces
of misery, the very misery
which comes before a wrath that will sweep us
all away
that I saw nothing more. Now, Slift
I'll tell you what I really think
about this business of ours.

It can't go on like this, nothing but buying and
    selling
and one man coldly stripping off another's skin;
there are too many people bellowing with pain
more of them all the time.
What falls into our bloody cellars
is past all comfort:
when they get hold of us
they'll toss us out
like rotten fish. Not one of us
will die in bed. Before
we come to that they'll stand us against walls
mob after mob and clean the world of us and
our hangers-on.

Slift They've shaken you up!
(*aside*) I'll force a rare steak on him. His old weakness
has hit him again. Maybe he'll come to himself after
enjoying some raw meat. (*He goes and broils MAULER
a steak on a gas cooker*)

Mauler I often wonder why
        I'm stirred by those goofy transcendental speeches
        the cheap, flat jabber they bone up.
        It must be because they do it free and eighteen
            hours a day and
        in rain and hunger.

Slift In cities that are burning from below
        and freezing on the top, there are always those
        who'll talk of this and that, details that aren't
        in perfect order.

Mauler But what are they saying? If in these cities
            ceaselessly
        burning, amid the downward rush
        of bellowing humanity, surging
        year after year without a break
        to hell, I hear a voice like that
        foolish of course, but not at all beastly
        I feel as though I'd been cracked on the backbone

       with a stick, like a leaping fish.
       But that's been mere evasion up to now, Slift.
       What I fear isn't God but something else.

Slift   What is it?

Mauler   Not what's above but
       what's below me! What stands in the stockyards
         and can't
       last the night and yet, I know, will
       rise in the morning.

Slift   Pierpont, my friend, won't you eat a piece of meat?
Think: now you can, for your conscience is clear. As of
today you have nothing to do with cattle-murder.

Mauler   You think I could? Maybe I should.
       I should be able to now, shouldn't I?

Slift   Eat something and consider your situation, which is
not very good. Do you realize that today you bought up all
there is inside tin cans?

    Mauler, I see you engrossed in contemplating your
noble nature, allow me to give you a concise account of
your situation, the wholly external, unimportant one.

    The main point is that you've taken a hundred and fifty
tons of reserve stocks away from the meat ring. You'll
have to unload these during the next few weeks on a
market that can't swallow another can as it is. You paid
50 for them, but the price will go down to at least 30. On
November 15, when the price is 30 or 25, the meat ring will
deliver four hundred tons to you at 50.

Mauler   Slift, I am lost!
       This is the end. I've gone and bought up meat.
       Oh, Slift, what have I done!
       Slift, I've loaded myself with all the meat in the
         world.
       Like Atlas, cans by the ton on my shoulders
       I stumble down to join the hoboes. Only this
         morning
       many men were about to fall and I
       went to see them fall and laugh at them

and tell them no one now
would be fool enough to buy meat in cans
and as I stand there I hear my own voice say:
I'll buy it all.
Slift, I've gone and bought meat, I'm ruined.

Slift Well, what do you hear from your friends in New York?

Mauler That I should buy meat.

Slift You should do what?

Mauler Buy meat.

Slift Then why are you moaning because you've bought it?

Mauler Yes, they told me I should buy meat.

Slift But you have bought meat!

Mauler That's right, I did buy meat, but I bought it
not because of the letter that said I should
(which is all wrong anyway, just abstract
theory) not from base motives, but because
that person gave me such a shock. I swear
I barely riffled through the letter, it came this
morning.
Here it is. "Dear Pierpont,"

Slift (*reads on*) "today we are able to inform you that our
money is beginning to bear fruit. Many Congressmen are
going to vote against tariffs. So it seems advisable to buy
meat, dear Pierpont. We shall write you again tomorrow."

Mauler Bribery is something else
that shouldn't happen. How easily
a war could start that way and thousands bleed
for filthy lucre. Slift, my friend, I feel
no good can come of news like this.

Slift It would depend who wrote the letter.
Bribing, repealing tariffs, making wars
aren't for just anyone. Are these good people?

Mauler Solvent people.

Slift But who? (*MAULER smiles*) So prices might rise after
all?
Then we'd be off the hook. This could improve
our prospects if it wasn't for all that meat

the farmers have: only too greedily offered
it will bring prices crashing down again.
Mauler, I don't understand that letter.

Mauler   Look at it this way. A man has stolen something
and is caught by a man.
Now, if he doesn't knock the fellow down
he's lost, but if he does, he's out of the woods.
The letter (which is wrong) demands (so as to be
   right)
a crime like that.

Slift   What crime?

Mauler   A kind I can never commit. From this day on
I wish to live in peace. If they want to profit
by their crimes, and profit they will
they have only to buy meat wherever they can
   get it
impress the fact upon the stockbreeders
that there's too much meat around and mention
the Lennox shutdown and take
their meat away. This above all:
take the stockbreeders' meat from them, but then
they'll be betrayed again, no, I'll have nothing
to do with that.

Slift   Pierpont, you shouldn't have bought that meat.

Mauler   Yes, it's a bad deal, Slift.
I'm not going to buy a hat or a shoe until
I'm out of this affair. I'll be delighted
if I have a hundred dollars when it's over.

(*Drumming. JOAN enters with the STOCKBREEDERS*)

Joan   We'll lure him out of his den the way you catch a
cricket. You'd better stand over there, because if he hears
me singing he'll try to get out on the other side, so as not
to have to meet me again: he doesn't like to see me. (*She
laughs*) Or the people with me.

(*The STOCKBREEDERS go and stand outside door on
right*)

Joan   (*outside door on left*)   Please come out, Mr. Mauler,

I must talk to you about the miseries of the stockbreeders of Illinois. There are also several workers with me, who want to ask you when you're going to reopen your factory.

Mauler Slift, where's the other way out? I don't want to meet her again, and certainly not the people with her. And I'm not opening any factory now.

Slift Come out this way. (*They go through interior to door on right*)

Stockbreeders (*outside door on right*) Come on out, Mauler. Our troubles are all your fault, and we're more than ten thousand Illinois stockbreeders, at our wits' end. So buy our livestock from us.

Mauler Shut the door, Slift! I'm not buying.

With the whole world's canned meat around my
  neck
shall I now buy the livestock on the Dog Star?
It's as if someone should say to Atlas when
he can barely manage to drag the world along:
"They need another carrier on Saturn."
Who's going to buy the livestock back from me?

Slift The Grahams, if anybody will. They need it.

Joan (*outside door on left*) We're not going to leave till the stockbreeders are helped too.

Mauler The Grahams, if anybody, yes, they need livestock. Slift, go out and tell them to give me a couple of minutes to think (*SLIFT goes*)

Slift (*to the STOCKBREEDERS*) Pierpont Mauler wishes to weigh your request. He asks for two minutes' thinking time. (*He comes back in*)

Mauler I'm not buying. (*He begins to calculate*) Slift, I'm buying. Slift, bring me whatever looks like a hog or a steer, I'll buy it, whatever smells of lard, I'll buy it, bring every grease-spot, I'm the buyer, and that at today's price, 50.

Slift You're not going to buy a hat, Mauler, just all the livestock in Illinois.

Mauler Yes, that's what I'm buying. Now it's settled, Slift.

Take A. (*He draws an A on a closet door*)
A man makes a mistake, let that be A
he did it because his feelings overcame him
and now he goes and does B, and B's wrong too
and now the sum of A and B is right.
Let the stockbreeders in, they are good people
badly off and decently dressed and not
the kind that scare you when you see them.

Slift (*comes out in front of the house; to the STOCK-BREEDERS*) To save Illinois and avert the ruin of its farmers and stockbreeders, Pierpont Mauler has decided to buy up all the livestock on the market.

Stockbreeders   Hurrah for Pierpont Mauler! He's saved the cattle trade! (*They enter the house*)

Joan (*calls after them*)   Tell Mr. Mauler that we, the Black Straw Hats, thank him for this in the name of God. (*to the WORKERS*) If the people who buy livestock and the people who sell it are satisfied, there'll be bread once again for you too.

VII

THE TRADERS DRIVEN OUT OF THE TEMPLE

The Black Straw Hat Mission. The BLACK STRAW HATS, sitting at a long table, are counting out from their tin boxes the widows' and orphans' mites they have collected.

Black Straw Hats (*singing*)   Sing as ye gather the pennies
            of widows and orphans now!
      Their need is dire
      They have no bread, no fire
      but our Almighty Sire
      will feed them too, somehow.

Paulus Snyder, Major of the Black Straw Hats (*getting up*)
Not much, not much! (*to several POOR PEOPLE in the
background, including MRS. LUCKERNIDDLE and
GLOOMB*) You here again? Aren't you ever going to
leave? There's work in the stockyards again, you know!

Mrs. Luckerniddle Oh? Where? The yards are closed.

Gloomb The story was that they were going to open, but
they haven't.

Snyder Well, don't go too near the cash-box. (*He waves
them still farther back*)
(*MULBERRY, the landlord, enters*)

Mulberry Come on, what about my rent?

Snyder Beloved Black Straw Hats, good friend Mulberry,
most honored listeners! As regards the troublesome
problem of financing our operations—a good thing speaks
for itself, and what it needs most is propaganda—we have
hitherto turned to the poor, indeed the poorest of the
poor, in the belief that those in greatest need of God's
help would most likely have something left over for Him,
and that sheer numbers would do the trick. Alas,
experience has taught us that these very levels of society
are mysteriously aloof from God. This, however, may be
due to the fact that they have nothing. Therefore I, Paulus
Snyder, have issued an invitation in your name to the rich
and prosperous men of Chicago to help us launch a major
offensive next Saturday against the unbelief and
materialism of the city of Chicago, principally against the
lowest levels. A part of this money will go to our good
landlord, Mr. Mulberry, in payment of the rent he is so
kindly deferring.

Mulberry It would certainly be welcome, but don't let it
worry you. (*He leaves*)

Snyder Now, then, go happily about your work and be sure
to clean the front steps.
(*The BLACK STRAW HATS leave*)

Snyder (*to the POOR PEOPLE*) Tell me: are the locked-out
workers still standing patiently in the stockyards or have
they started to talk rebellion?

Mrs. Luckerniddle They've been raising a howl since yesterday, because they know the factories are getting orders.

Gloomb A lot of them are saying there won't be any more work at all unless force is used.

Snyder (*to himself*) A good sign. The meat kings will be gladder to come and listen to our appeal if they're driven in by stones. (*to the POOR PEOPLE*) Couldn't you split our wood, at least?

Poor People There isn't any more wood, Major.

(*CRIDLE, GRAHAM, SLIFT, MEYERS enter*)

Meyers Graham, I wonder: where's that livestock hiding?

Graham That's what I wonder too. Where's the livestock hiding?

Slift I wonder, too.

Graham You, too? And Mauler wonders too, no doubt?

Slift Mauler too, no doubt.

Meyers Somewhere some hog is buying everything up.
And that hog knows quite well that we're committed
by contract to deliver meat in cans
and so we need the livestock.

Slift Who can it be?

Graham (*hitting SLIFT in the pit of the stomach*) You dirty dog!
Don't play any tricks on us there, and tell Pierpy not to either!
That's a vital spot!

Slift (*to SNYDER*) What do you want of us?

Graham (*hitting him again*) What do you think they want, Slift?

(*With overdone slyness SLIFT makes the gesture of handing out money*)

Graham You said it, Slift!

Myers (*to SNYDER*) Fire away. (*The FOUR take seats in the pews*)

Snyder (*in the pulpit*) We Black Straw Hats have heard that there are fifty thousand men standing around in the stockyards without any work. And that some are

grumbling and saying: "We'll have to help ourselves."
Aren't you being named as those whose fault it is that the
fifty thousand have no work and are standing in front of
the factories? If this keeps up, they'll take the factories
away from you and say: "We'll do as the Bolsheviks did
and take over the factories ourselves, so that everyone
can work and eat." You see, the story is getting around
that unhappiness doesn't just come like the rain, but is
made by certain people who profit by it. But we Black
Straw Hats want to tell them that unhappiness does fall
like the rain, nobody knows where from, and that suffering
is their fate and a reward for it awaits them.

Packers Why talk of rewards?

Snyder The reward we talk of is paid out after death.

Packers How much do you want for this?

Snyder Eight hundred dollars a month, because we need
hot soup and loud music. We also want to promise them
that the rich will be punished—when they're dead, of
course. (*The PACKERS guffaw*) And all this for only eight
hundred dollars a month!

Graham You don't need that much, man. Five hundred!

Snyder We could get by on seven hundred and fifty, but
then—

Meyers Seven hundred and fifty. That's better. Let's make
it five hundred.

Graham You need five hundred, that's for sure. (*to the
others*) They've got to have that.

Meyers (*front*) Out with it, Slift, you fellows have that
livestock.

Slift Mauler and I have not bought a penny's worth of
livestock, as true as I sit here. The Lord's my witness.

Meyers (*to SNYDER*) Five hundred dollars? That's a lot of
money. Who's going to pay it?

Slift Yes, indeed. Now you'll have to find someone who'll
give it to you.

Snyder Yes, yes.

Meyers That won't be easy.

Graham   Spill it, Slift! Pierpy has that livestock.

Slift (*laughs*)   Bunch of crooks, Mr. Snyder. (*All laugh except SNYDER*)

Graham (*to MEYERS*)   Don't like the man. No sense of humor.

Slift   Here's the main point, man. Where do you stand? This side of the barricades, or the other?

Snyder   The Black Straw Hats stand above the battle, Mr. Slift. This side.

(*JOAN enters*)

Slift   Here's our Saint Joan of the Livestock Exchange!

Packers (*bellowing at JOAN*)   Listen: we're not satisfied with you. Can't you straighten something out for us with Mauler? People say you have influence there. He's supposed to be your pet. The market's so short of livestock that we've got to keep an eye on him. They say you can wrap him round your little finger. So tell him to trot out that livestock. Listen: if you do this for us we're willing to pay the Black Straw Hats' rent for four years.

(*JOAN has seen the POOR PEOPLE and is shocked*)

Mrs. Luckerniddle (*comes forward*)

> The twenty lunches have been eaten. Don't
> let it enrage you now to see me here.
> I would gladly free you from the sight of me.
> Hunger is a cruel thing: whenever
> you satisfy it, back it comes again.

Gloomb (*coming forward*)

> I know you, it was you I tried to talk
> into working on the slicer that tore my arm off.
> Today I could do worse things than that.

Joan   Why aren't you working? I did get work for you.

Mrs. Luckerniddle   Oh? Where? The stockyards are closed.

Gloomb   The story was that they were going to open, but they haven't.

Joan (*to the PACKERS*)   So they're still waiting, are they? (*The PACKERS are silent*)

> And I thought they had been relieved!

For seven days the snow has fallen on them
and the very snow that kills them withdraws them
from every human eye. How easily
I forgot what everyone gladly forgets and then
    finds peace.
If anyone says "It's over," he goes unquestioned.
(*to the PACKERS*) Surely Mauler bought meat from you?
    He did it
    because I stood up for you! And now you still
    refuse
    to open your plants?

Packers   That's right, we did want to open up.

Slift   But first you wanted to leap at the farmers' throats!

Packers   How can we slaughter when there's no livestock to be had?

Slift   Mauler and I bought meat from you on the assumption that you would get work going so the worker could buy meat. Now who's supposed to eat the meat we took off your hands? For whom did we buy meat, I ask you, if the eaters can't pay?

Joan   Seeing that you people have control of all the equipment your employees use in your high and mighty factories and plants, the least you could do would be to let them get at it, or else they're utterly done for, because there is really a kind of exploitation in this, and if a poor human creature, tormented till the blood comes, can think of no way out but to take a club and bash his tormentor on the head, then you wet your pants, and then religion looks good again and it's expected to calm things down, but the Lord has His pride too, and He's not about to let you off and clean your pigsty for you. And I go running from Gog to Magog and think: if I help you people up above, the ones beneath you will also be helped. It's all one in a way, and the same strings pull it. But I was a prize fool there. If a man wants to help folks that are poor it seems he'd better help them get away from you. Have you lost all respect for whatever wears a human face?

Some day you may not be looked upon as human beings either, but as wild beasts that will have to be slaughtered in the interest of public order and security! And still you dare to enter the house of God, just because you have that filthy Mammon, everybody knows where you got it and how, it wasn't honestly earned. But this time, by God, you've come to the wrong address, we'll have to drive you out, that's it, drive you out with a stick. Don't give me that dumb look, men shouldn't be treated like steers, but you aren't men, get out of here fast or I'll lay my hands on you, don't hold me back, I know what I'm doing, I was in the dark too long.

(*She drives them out with an inverted flag, using it as a stick. The BLACK STRAW HATS appear at the doors*)

Joan   Out! Are you trying to turn God's house into a barn? A second Livestock Exchange? Out! There's nothing for you here. Faces like yours aren't wanted here. You're undeserving and I'm showing you the door. For all your money!

Packers   All right. But forty months' rent goes with us— plainly, modestly, irrevocably. We can't spare a penny, anyhow. We face times as terrible as the cattle market has ever seen. (*They leave with SLIFT*)

Snyder (*running after them*)   Please stay, gentlemen, don't leave, she has no authority at all! A crazy female! She'll be fired! She'll get you anything you want.

Joan (*to the BLACK STRAW HATS*)   This does make things awkward, what with the rent and all. But we can't think about that now. (*to MRS. LUCKERNIDDLE and GLOOMB*) Sit back there, I'll bring you some soup.

Snyder (*returning*)   That's right, ask the poor to dinner
          and treat them to rainwater and fine words
          when even up above there is no pity for them
          but only snow!
          Without any humility
          you followed your first impulse! It's so much easier
          just to drive the unclean away in arrogance.

You're squeamish about the bread we have to eat.
All too curious how it's made and still you want
to keep on eating! Go, thou celestial one
out in the rain and abide in righteousness in the
   blizzard!

Joan   Does that mean I'm to take off my uniform?

Snyder   Take off your uniform and pack your bag! Leave
this house and take along the riffraff you brought in.
Nothing but riffraff and scum followed you in here. Now
you'll belong to it yourself. Get your things.
(*JOAN goes and returns dressed like a country
maidservant, carrying a valise*)

Joan   I'll go find rich man Mauler, who is not
   without fear or good will, and ask
   him to help us. Not earlier shall I
   once more put on this coat and black straw hat
   nor earlier return to this beloved house
   of songs and awakenings than
   I bring rich Mauler back with me
   as one of us, thoroughly converted.
   What if their money like a cancerous ulcer
   has eaten up their ears and human faces
   so that they sit apart, but loftily
   beyond the reach of any cry for help!
   Poor cripples!
   There must be *one* just man among them! (*She
      leaves*)

Snyder   Poor simpleton!
   You're blind to this: set up in huge formations
   givers and takers of work
   face one another:
   warring fronts, irreconcilable.
   Run back and forth between them, reconciler,
      mediator
   be useful to neither and perish.

Mulberry (*enters*)   Have you the money now?

Snyder   God will still be able to pay for the definitely scanty shelter He has found on earth, I said scanty, Mr. Mulberry.

Mulberry Yes, pay, you bet, that's what it's all about! You
said it, Snyder! If the Lord pays, fine. But if He don't pay,
not so fine. If the Lord don't pay His rent He's got to go,
and that'll be Saturday night, eh, Snyder? (*He leaves*)

VIII

PIERPONT MAULER'S SPEECH ON THE
INDISPENSABILITY OF CAPITALISM
AND RELIGION

Mauler's office.

Mauler Now, Slift, the day has come
    when our good Graham and all the others who
      were planning
    to wait with him for the lowest livestock price
    must buy the meat they owe us.

Slift They'll buy it dearer, because any cattle
    bellowing today in the Chicago market
    are our cattle.
    And every hog they owe us they will have
    to buy from us and it's expensive there.

Mauler And now, Slift, let loose all your wholesalers!
    Tell them to pester the livestock market with
      demands
    for whatever looks at all like hogs or cattle
    so that the price will rise.

Slift What news of your Joan? On the livestock market
    there is a rumor that you slept with her.
    I contradicted it. Since the time she
    threw us all out of the temple she hasn't been
      heard of.

It's as if black bellowing Chicago had swallowed
her.

Mauler I like her action very much, throwing you out
just like that. The girl's afraid of nothing
and if I too had been there when it happened
she'd have thrown me out too and I like her for it
and also I like that house of hers because
people of my sort are not possible there.
Slift, hike the price to 80, then those Grahams
will be something like mud that you stick your foot
in
just to have another look at its shape.
I won't let an ounce of meat get loose, so that
this time I can skin them once for all
in my natural manner.

Slift Mauler, I'm glad to see you've shaken off
your weakness of the last few days. And now
I'll go watch them buy up livestock. (*He leaves*)

Mauler It's high time this damn town had its skin ripped off
and somebody taught those fellows a thing or two
about the meat business, even if it makes them
yell "Crime!"

(*JOAN enters with her valise*)

Joan Hello, Mr. Mauler. You're a hard man to find. I'll put
my things here for the time being. You see, I'm not with
the Black Straw Hats any more. There were
disagreements. So I thought, well, I'll go see how Mr.
Mauler's getting along. With none of that nagging mission
work to do, I can pay more attention to the individual
human being. So now I'll concern myself a bit with you, if
you'll let me, that is. You know, I've noticed something:
you're more approachable, more than many another. That's
a fine old mohair sofa you have there, but why do you
have a sheet on it? It's not made up right, either. So you
sleep in your office, do you? I thought surely you would
have one of those great big palaces. (*MAULER is silent*)
But you're right. Mr. Mauler, to be a good manager in
little things as well, being a meat king. I don't know why,

but when I see you I always think of the story about the
Lord when He visits Adam in the Garden of Eden and He
calleth out "Adam, where art thou?" Do you know it still?
(*laughs*) Adam's standing behind a bush again, with his
arms in a doe again, up to the elbows as it were, and so,
all bloody, he hears the voice of God. So he really acts
as if he wasn't there. But God stands firm and looks into
the matter and calleth once again: "Adam, where art
thou?" And then Adam says very faintly and blushing a
fiery red: "This is the time you pick to visit me, right after
I killed the doe. Don't say a word, I know I shouldn't have
done it." But your conscience is clear, Mr. Mauler, I hope.

Mauler So you're not with the Black Straw Hats any more?

Joan No, Mr. Mauler, and I don't belong there either.

Mauler Then what have you been living on? (*JOAN is
silent*) I see. Nothing. How long is it since you left the
Black Straw Hats?

Joan Eight days.

Mauler (*aside, tearfully*)   So greatly changed, and in only
   eight days!
   Where has she been? To whom has she been
    talking? What was it
   that drew those lines around her mouth?
   The city this girl comes from
   I do not yet know. (*He brings food on a tray*)
   You're greatly changed, my dear. Something to
    eat?
   I'm not eating. (*JOAN looks at the food*)

Joan Mr. Mauler, after we drove the rich people out of our
house—

Mauler Which amused me very much, and seemed the right
things to do—

Joan the landlord, who lives on the rent, gave us notice for
next Sunday.

Mauler So the Black Straw Hats are badly off financially?

Joan Yes, and that's why I thought I'd go see Mr. Mauler.
(*She begins to eat greedily*)

Mauler Don't worry. I'll go into the market and get you the

money you need. Yes, I'll do that for you too, I'll raise it,
cost what it may, even if I have to slice it right out of this
town's skin. For you people I'll do it. Money's expensive,
of course, but I'll raise it. That will suit you.

Joan Yes, Mr. Mauler.

Mauler So go and tell them the money's coming, it'll be
there by Saturday. Mauler's raising it. He just now left to
raise it on the livestock market. That matter of the fifty
thousand went badly, not entirely as desired. I couldn't get
them work right away. But yours is a different case, my
dear, and your Black Straw Hats shall be spared, I'll get
the money for them. Run and tell them.

Joan Yes, Mr. Mauler!

Mauler There, I've put it in writing. Take it.

> I too regret that they are waiting for work
> in the stockyards and not very good work at that.
> Fifty thousand men
> standing around in the yards, not even leaving at
>   night! *(JOAN stops eating)*
> But that's the way this business goes:
> it's to be or not to be, a question whether
> I am to be the best man in my class
> or take the dark road down to the yards myself.
> Besides, the scum is filling them up again and
> making trouble.
> And now, I'll say it frankly, I would have liked
> to hear from you that what I do is right
> and my business natural: therefore
> assure me it was your advice I followed
> in ordering meat from the meat ring and from
> the stockbreeders too, thus doing good and
> since I'm well aware that you're poor and right now
> they're trying to take away the roof over your heads
> I want to add a contribution for that: as proof
> of my good will.

Joan Then the workers are still waiting outside the
slaughterhouses?

Mauler   Why are you against money? and look
        so very different when you haven't any?
        What do you think about money? You must
        tell me, I want to know, and not think wrongly
        the way a fool will think of money as
        a thing to be doubted. Consider reality and
        plain truth, perhaps not pleasant but
        true for all that: everything is unsteady and the
           human race
        almost at the mercy of chance, of the weather
        but money's a means of making some
           improvements, maybe
        only for some, but all the same: what a structure!
        Erected from time immemorial, over and over again
        because it keeps collapsing, yet tremendous,
           though demanding
        sacrifice, very hard to set up and continually
        set up with groans but inescapably
        wresting the possible from a reluctant planet,
           however
        much or little that may be, and therefore constantly
        defended by the best. Just think: if I
        who have much against it and sleep badly, should
        attempt to leave it, it would be as if
        a fly stopped holding back an avalanche.
        I would become a nothing and it would keep on
           going over me.
        Otherwise everything would have to be utterly
           overthrown
        and the blueprint totally changed to suit
        a new, quite different, fantastic estimate of man,
           wanted
        neither by you nor us, for this would happen
        without us or God, who would lose His function
           and be dismissed.
        So you must work with us, and even if you make
           no sacrifices, which

we wouldn't ask of you anyhow, still approve the
sacrifices.
In a word, you must
set up God once more
the only salvation and
beat the drum for Him so that He may
find a footing in the districts of misery and His
voice may resound in the stockyards.
That would be enough. (*He holds out the note to
her*)
Take what you get, but know the reason and
then take it! Here's the voucher for four years' rent.

Joan Mr. Mauler, I don't understand what you've been
saying
and I don't want to either. (*She stands up*)
I know it should delight me now to hear
that God is to be helped, but I belong
with those who are
not helped that way. And who are offered nothing.

Mauler If you bring the Straw Hats the money you can also
stay in their house again. Living on nothing
isn't good for you, my dear. Believe me
they're out for money; and so they should be.

Joan If the Black Straw Hats
accept your money, they are welcome to it
but I will take my stand among the people waiting
in the yards
until the factories are open again and
eat nothing but what they eat and if
snow is what they get, then snow, and the work
they do I will do also, because I have
no money either and no other way to get it, not
honestly
at least, and if there's no work, then let there be
none for me either and
you, sir, who live on poverty and
can't look at the poor and condemn

something you don't know and arrange
not to see what sits condemned
abandoned in the stockyards, unbeheld:
If you want to see me again
come to the stockyards. (*She leaves*)

Mauler Tonight then, get up
every hour, Mauler, and
look out of the window to see if it's snowing, and
   if it is
it will be snowing on the girl you know.

IX

JOAN'S THIRD DESCENT INTO THE DEPTHS: THE SNOWFALL

Stockyards district.

Joan Listen to the dream I had one night
   a week ago.
Before me in a little field, too little
for the shade of an average tree, because it was
hemmed in by enormous houses, I saw a mass
of people, I couldn't make out how many, but
far more than the sparrows that so small a space
could hold, a very thick mass therefore, so that
the field buckled, rose in the middle and the mass
hung on the edge, holding fast
a moment, throbbing within, then
at the visitation of a word, shouted somewhere
with casual intent, it began to flow.
Now I saw columns, streets, familiar ones,
   Chicago! you!
I saw you marching, then I saw myself.

Saw myself striding mutely at your head
with warrior steps and blood upon my brow
and shouting words that sounded warlike
in a tongue I didn't know, and since many columns
were marching at the same time from many
   directions
I strode in multiple form at the head of many
   columns
young and old, sobbing and cursing
beside myself at last! Virtue and terror!
Transforming whatever my foot touched, bringing
   to pass
measureless destruction, visibly influencing
the courses of the stars but also radically changing
the streets close by, known to us all—
so moved the column and I with it
veiled by snow from any hostile attack
transparent with hunger, no target
strikable nowhere, being settled nowhere
unreachable by any torment, being used
to all. And so it marches, abandoning
the untenable position, taking any it can find.
That was my dream.
Today I see the meaning.
Before day breaks we shall
set out from these yards and
reach their city Chicago in the dawn
showing in public places the full extent of our
   misery
appealing to anything with a human look.
What will come after, I don't know.

Livestock Exchange.
Mauler (*to the PACKERS*)

My friends in New York have written me
that the tariff law to the south of us
has fallen today.

Packers   Horror, the tariff fallen and we
            have no meat to sell! It's been sold already
            at a low price and now we're supposed to buy meat
               when it's rising!
Stockbreeders   Horror, the tariff fallen and we
            have no cattle to sell! It's been sold already
            at a low price!
Small Speculators   Horror! Ever inscrutable
            are the eternal laws
            of human economics!
            Without warning
            the volcano opens up and lays the country waste!
            Without an invitation
            the profitable island rises from the barren seas!
            No one is told, no one is in the know! But the
               hindmost
            is bitten by the dogs!
Mauler   Seeing that livestock's in demand
            in cans at an acceptable price
            I request that you deliver to me now
            and fast the meat I must obtain from you
            as stated in the contract.
Graham   At the old price?
Mauler   As was agreed, Graham.
            Four hundred tons, if I remember correctly
            a moment when I was not in my right mind.
Packers   How can we take on livestock now, with prices
               rising?
            There's someone who has cornered it, a man
            whom no one knows—
            Mauler, you must release us from the contract!
Mauler   My regrets, but I must have those cans. There's still
            livestock enough, a touch expensive, sure, but
            livestock enough. Buy it up!
Packers   Buy livestock now? Nuts to that!

Small tavern in the stockyards district. Male and female

*WORKERS, JOAN among them. A troop of BLACK STRAW
HATS comes in. JOAN gets up and gestures at them
frantically during what follows.*

Jackson (*after a hurried song*)

        Brother, why won't you eat the bread that Jesus
           gives?

        Lo, how joyful and glad are we.

        It's because we've found Christ Jesus, Lord of all
           our lives.

        You too, come to him speedily!

        Hallelujah!

*(A GIRL in the BLACK STRAW HATS speaks to the
WORKERS, making side remarks to her comrades)*

Black Straw Hat   (This is no use, is it?) Brothers and
sisters, once I too, like you, stood sadly by the roadside,
and the old Adam in me wanted nothing but to eat and
drink, but then I found my Lord Jesus, and then came the
light and I was glad and now (they aren't even listening!) if I
just think good and hard about my Lord Jesus, who in His
pain redeemed us all, despite our many misdeeds, why,
I feel hunger and thirst no more, except for our Lord
Jesu's word. (It's no good.) Where the Lord Jesu is,
violence is not, but peace; hate is not, but love. (It's all a
waste.)

Black Straw Hats   Hallelujah!

*(JACKSON passes the box around. But nothing is put into
it)*

        Hallelujah!

Joan   Oh, why must they be such a nuisance here

        in the cold, and talk on top of it?

        Really, I can hardly

        bear to hear the words

        that once were dear and pleasant to me! Why
          doesn't

        a voice, a vestige in them, say to them: Here is
        snow and wind, be silent!

Woman   Just let her be. Those people have to do that if

they want to get a bit of warmth and food at the mission.
Wish I was there too!

Mrs. Luckerniddle   That was nice music!

Gloomb   Nice and short.

Mrs. Luckerniddle   But they really are good people.

Gloomb   Good and short, short and sweet.

Female Worker   Why don't they give us a real talk and
convert us?

Gloomb (*mimics paying out money*)   Can you keep the pot
boiling, Mrs. Swingurn?

Female Worker   The music's very pretty, but I expected
them to give us a plate of soup, maybe, since they had
a pot along.

Worker   No kidding, you thought that?

Joan   Are there no people here with any enterprise?

A Worker   Yes, the Communists.

Joan   Aren't they people who incite to crime?

The Worker   No.

Livestock Exchange.

Packers   We're buying livestock! Yearlings!
Feeders! Calves! Steers! Hogs!
We invite offers!

Stockbreeders   Nothing's left! Whatever was saleable
we have sold.

Packers   Nothing? And the depots
are jammed with livestock.

Stockbreeders   Sold.

Packers   Sold to whom? (*MAULER enters*)

Packers (*mobbing him*)   Not a steer to be dug up in
Chicago!
You must grant us a delay, Mauler.

Mauler   Nothing doing. You'll deliver your meat. (*He goes
over to SLIFT*)
Squeeze 'em dry.

A Stockbreeder   Eight hundred Kentucky steers at 400.

Packers   Impossible. Are you crazy? 400?

Slift I'll take them. 400.

Stockbreeders Eight hundred steers to Sullivan Slift at 400.

Packers It's Mauler! What did we say? He's the one!

You dirty crook, he's forcing us to deliver canned
  meat to him

and buying up cattle! So we have to buy the meat
  from him

that we need to fill his cans!

You filthy butcher! Here, take *our* flesh, hack off
  a slice!

Mauler If someone's a steer he shouldn't be surprised if it
makes people hungry to look at him.

Graham (*ready to attack MAULER*) He's got to go, I'll finish
him!

Mauler All right, Graham. Now I demand your cans!

You can stuff yourself into them.

I'll teach you the meat business, you

traders! From now on every hoof, every calf from
  here

to Illinois is paid to my account, and dearly

and so, for a start, I offer five hundred steers at
  56. (*pause*)

Well, as demand is poor, since nobody here needs
  livestock

I'll make it 60! And don't forget
my cans!

*Another part of the stockyards. Signboards read: Keep
solidarity with the locked-out stockyards workers! All out
for the general strike! Outside a shed TWO MEN from
the central union office are talking with a group of
WORKERS. JOAN enters.*

Joan Are these the leaders in the cause of the
unemployed? I can help too. I've learned to speak in
streets and meeting-halls, even big ones. I'm not
afraid of insults, and can find good words, I think, for a
good cause. I really think something's got to happen, and
soon. Also, I have suggestions to make.

A Workers' Leader Listen, everybody. Up to now the meat crowd have not shown the least inclination to reopen their plants. At first, it looked as if the exploiter Pierpont Mauler was pushing for a reopening, since he's been demanding from the meat crowd huge amounts of canned meat that they owe him by contract. Then it came out that the meat they need for packing is in Mauler's own hands, and he has no intention to let it go. Now we know: if it's up to the meat crowd we workers will never all be able to return to the slaughterhouses, and never again at the old wage. In this state of affairs we must realize that only the use of force can help us. The city utilities have promised us now that they will join the general strike by the day after tomorrow, at latest. This piece of news must be broadcast in every section of the stockyards, now, because without it there's a danger that the masses will be led by some rumor or other to leave the yards, and then they'll have to yield to the meat crowd's conditions. So these letters, stating that the gasworks, waterworks and power stations are willing to help us by going on strike, must be handed to the delegates who will be waiting for our passwords at ten tonight in different sections of the yards. Stick that in your overalls, Jack, and wait for the delegates outside Mother Schmitt's canteen! (*A WORKER takes the letter and leaves*)

Second Worker Give me the one for the Graham plant, I know it.

Workers' Leader 26th Street, corner Michigan Park. (*The WORKER takes the letter and leaves*) 13th Street, by the Westinghouse Building. (*to JOAN*) And who are you, girl?

Joan I was fired from the job I had.

Leader What kind of job was that?

Joan Selling a newspaper.

Leader Who were you working for?

Joan I'm a peddler.

A Worker Maybe she's a stool-pigeon.

Second Workers' Leader Who can tell what she'll do with the letter we give her?

First Leader No one.

> (*to JOAN*) The net with one mesh torn
> has no more use:
> the fish swim through it at that point
> as if no net were there.
> All the meshes
> are suddenly useless.

Joan I used to sell papers on 44th Street. I'm no stool-pigeon. I'm for your cause, heart and soul.

Second Leader Our cause? So it isn't your cause?

Joan It's certainly not in the public interest for the owners to put so many people in the street, just like that. It makes you think the poverty of the poor is useful to the rich! Poverty is all their doing, it would seem! (*uproarious laughter among the workers*) It's inhuman, that's what! And I mean even people like Mr. Mauler. (*renewed laughter*) Why do you laugh? I don't approve your malice, or your willingness to believe without proof that a man like Mr. Mauler could be inhuman.

Second Leader Not without proof. You can give her the letter, all right.

First Leader (*giving her the letter*) Go to Gate 5 at the Graham plant. If you see three workers come up and look around, ask if they're from the Cridle plant. The letter is for them.

Livestock Exchange.

Small Speculators Quotations dropping! The packing
> plants in peril!
> What will become of us, the stockholders?
> The man with modest savings who gave his all
> to a middle class that's weakened as it is?
> A man like Graham should be torn to bits
> before he makes waste paper of the note
> with our share marked on it, the one

we earned from his bloody cellars.
  Buy your livestock, buy it at any price!
*(At rear, throughout this scene, the names of firms
suspending payments are called out. "Suspending
payment: Meyer and Company," etc.)*

Packers We've had it, the price is over 70.

Wholesalers Knock 'em flat, the big shots aren't buying.

Packers Two thousand steers wanted at 70.

Slift *(to MAULER, by a pillar)* Push 'em up.

Mauler I see that you have not observed the terms
         of the contract I drew up with you that day
         in my desire to create employment. And now
             I hear
         they're still standing out there in the yards. Now
         you'll regret it: out with the canned meat
         which I have bought!

Graham We could do nothing; meat has disappeared
         totally from the market!
         Five hundred steers at 75.

Small Speculators Buy them, you bloody brutes!
         They won't buy! They'd rather give up
         the packing plants.

Mauler We shouldn't push it any higher, Slift.
         They've reached their limit now.
         Bleed they shall, but perish they must not:
         if they go we're goners too.

Slift There's life in 'em yet, push 'em higher.
         Five hundred steers at 77.

Small Speculators 77. Hear that? Why
         didn't you buy at 75? Now
         it's up to 77 and still climbing.

Packers We get 50 from Mauler for the cans and can't
    pay Mauler 80 for the cattle.

Mauler *(asking around)* Where are the people I sent to
    the stockyards?

A Man There's one.

Mauler Well, let's have it.

First Detective (*reporting*)   Sir, those crowds stretch
further than the eye can reach. If a person called out
for a Joan, maybe ten or a hundred would answer. They
sit and wait and have no face or name. Besides, one
man's voice alone cannot be heard, and far too many
people are running around asking for relatives they've
lost. In areas where the unions are active, grave unrest
prevails.

Mauler   Who's active? The unions? And the police let
them agitate? Damn it, go phone the police right away,
mention my name, ask them what we're paying taxes for.
Insist that the troublemakers get their heads cracked,
don't mince words. (*FIRST DETECTIVE leaves*)

Graham   All right then, Mauler, if we've got to go
give us a thousand at 77. We're through.

Slift   Five hundred to Graham at 77. All the rest at 80.

Mauler   Slift, this business isn't fun any more.
It could go too far. Keep on
up to 80, then let it go at 80.
I'll hand it over and let them off.
Enough's enough. The town needs
a breathing-spell. And I have other worries.
Slift, this throttling isn't as much
fun for me as I thought it would be.
(*He sees the SECOND DETECTIVE*)   Did you find her?

Second Detective   No, I saw no woman in a Black Straw
Hat uniform. There are a hundred thousand people
standing around in the yards, it's dark too, and the
biting wind drowns a man's shouts. Besides, the police
are clearing the yards and shooting has started.

Mauler   Shooting? At whom? Of course, I know.
It's strange; in this place nothing at all is heard.
And so she can't be found and there is shooting?
Go to the phone booths, look for Jim and tell him
not to call, or people will say again
that we're the ones who insisted on the shooting.
(*SECOND DETECTIVE leaves*)

Meyers Fifteen hundred at 80!

Slift Only five hundred at 80!

Meyers Five thousand at 80! Cutthroat!

Mauler Slift, I feel sick, leave off.

Slift Wouldn't think of it. There's life in 'em yet. And if
you weaken, Mauler, I'll push 'em higher.

Mauler Slift, I need some air. Carry on
with the dealing. I can't. Carry it on
as I would. I'd rather give everything away
than cause any more trouble! Don't
go higher than 85! But do things
as I would. You know me. (*He leaves*)

Slift Five hundred steers at 90!

Small Speculators We heard it, Mauler was willing
to settle for 85. Slift has no authority.

Slift That's a lie. I'll teach you
to sell meat in cans and
then have no meat!
Five thousand steers at 95! (*Uproar*)

Stockyards.   Many PEOPLE waiting, JOAN among them.

People Why are you sitting here?

Joan I have to hand over a letter. Three people are going
to come by here.   (*A group of REPORTERS enter,
led by a MAN*)

Man (*pointing at JOAN*)   That's the woman. (*to JOAN*)
These are reporters.

Reporters Hello, are you Joan Dark, the Black Straw
Hat girl?

Joan No.

Reporters We heard in Mr. Mauler's office that you've
sworn not to leave the stockyards until the packing
plants open. Here it is, you can read it in big letters on
the front page. (*JOAN turns away*)

Reporters (*reading aloud*)   Our Lady of the Slaughteryard,
Joan Dark, declares God keeps solidarity with
slaughterhouse workers.

Joan I said no such thing.

Reporters Miss Dark, we can tell you that public opinion is on your side. All Chicago feels with you, except for a few unscrupulous speculators. This means a terrific hit for your Black Straw Hats.

Joan I'm not with the Black Straw Hats any more.

Reporters Oh, come on, now. For us you belong to the Black Straw Hats. But we won't bother you, we'll stay in the background.

Joan I would like you to go away.   (*They sit down some way off*)

Workers (*at rear, in the stockyards*)
>   Until need is at its worst
>   they won't open the factories.
>   When misery has climbed
>   they will open up.
>   But they must answer us.
>   Don't leave until you have the answer.

Counter-Chorus (*also at rear*)
>   Wrong! No matter how high misery climbs
>   they won't open up
>   until their profit climbs.
>   If you wait for the answer
>   you will get the answer:
>   out of cannon and machine-guns
>   they will answer you.
>   And we advise you to wait
>   for this answer, that is, not to leave.

Joan I see this system and the way it looks
>   has long been known to me, but not
>   the way it hangs together! Some, a few, sit up
>   above
>   and many down below and the ones on top
>   shout down: Come up, so we'll all
>   be on top, but if you look closely you'll see
>   something covered between the ones above and
>   the ones below
>   that looks like a trail but it's no trail

> but a board and now you see it clearly
> it's a seesaw board, this whole system
> is a seesaw, with two ends that depend
> upon each other, and the ones on top
> sit up there only because the others sit below
> and only so long as the others sit below and
> they couldn't stay on top if the others came up
> leaving their place, so that
> they must desire that these shall sit below
> for all eternity and not come up.
> And there must be more below than up above
> or else the seesaw wouldn't hold. Yes, it's a
>   seesaw.

(*REPORTERS rise and move to rear, having received a piece of news*)

A Worker (*to JOAN*)   What have you got to do with those people?

Joan   Nothing.

Worker   But they were talking to you.

Joan   They took me for somebody else.

Old Man (*to JOAN*)   Say, you're mighty cold. Like a slug of whisky? (*Joan drinks*)   Hold it, hold it! That's no mean shot you swallowed!

A Woman   Shame on you!

Joan   Did you say something?

Woman   Yes, shame on you! Drinking up the old man's whisky!

Joan   Shut your trap, you silly creature. Hey, where's my shawl got to? They've gone and swiped it again. That's the limit! Swiping my shawl, on top of everything! Who's made off with my shawl? Give it back right now. (*She tears a sack off the head of the WOMAN standing beside her. The WOMAN defends herself*) Oh, so you're the one. No lies! Give me that sack.

The Woman   Help, she's killing me!

A Man   Shut up!

(*Someone flings a rag at her*)

Joan   For all you people care, I might be sitting around
in this draft bare naked.
It wasn't this cold in my dream. When I
came here with great plans, fortified
by dreams, I didn't dream that it could be
so cold here. Now what I miss most of all
is that warm scarf of mine. You people here
may well go hungry, you have nothing to eat
but for me they're waiting with a bowl of soup.
You may well be cold
but I can go any time
into the warm room
pick up the flag and beat the drum and talk
of Him who has His dwelling in the clouds.
What are you leaving? What I left
was no mere occupation but a calling
a noble habit, but a decent job
besides, with daily bread and shelter and support.
It seems to me almost like a play, beneath
my dignity, should I remain here
without dire need. And yet
I may not leave, and still—
I'll say it openly—I choke with fear
of this not eating, not sleeping, not knowing what
to do
habitual hunger, humiliating cold, and
above all, wanting to go away.

Workers   Stay here! Whatever happens
do not break ranks!
Only if you stay together
can you help each other!
Understand: you have been betrayed
by all your public spokesmen
and your unions, which are bought.
Listen to no one, believe nothing
but test every proposal
that leads to real change. And above all learn:

It will only work by force and
if you do it yourselves.

Reporters (*returning*)   Hello, girl, you've had a smashing
success: we've just learned that the millionaire Pierpont
Mauler, who has huge amounts of livestock in his hands,
is releasing livestock to the slaughterhouses in spite of
rising prices. In these circumstances work will resume
in the yards tomorrow.

Joan   What good news! The ice has melted in their hearts.
At least
the one just man among them
has not failed us. Approached as a human being
he answered humanly. So
goodness exists.   (*Machine-guns crackle in
the distance*)
What's that noise?

A Reporter   Those are army machine-guns. The army has
orders to clear the stockyards, because the agitators
who are inciting to violence will have to be silenced now
that the slaughterhouses are to be reopened.

A Worker (*to JOAN*)   Take it easy, stay where you are.
The stockyards are so big it'll take the army hours to
get here.

Joan   How many people are in them?

Reporters   There must be a hundred thousand.

Joan   So many?
Oh, what an unknown school, an unlawful space
thick with snow, where hunger is teacher and
unpreventably
need speaks about necessity.
A hundred thousand pupils, what are you learning?

Workers (*at rear*)   If you stay together
they will slaughter you.
We advise you to stay together!
If you fight
their tanks will crush you.
We advise you to fight!

This battle will be lost
and maybe the next one too
will be lost.
But you are learning to fight
and becoming aware
that it will only work by force and
if you do it yourselves.

Joan   Stop: no more lessons
so coldly learned!
Do not use force
to fight disorder and confusion.
Certainly the temptation is tremendous!
Another night like this, another such
wordless oppression and nobody
can stay at peace. And surely you have stood
together in many nights of many years
learning cold and terrible thoughts.
Certainly, too, outrage on outrage
fault upon fault is gathering in the dark
and unfinished business
is gathering.
But who will eat
the meal that's cooking here?
I'm going to leave. What's done by force cannot be good.
I don't belong to these people. If hunger and the tread of
misery had taught me force as a child, I'd belong to
them and ask no questions. As it is, I've got to leave.
(*She makes no move*)

Reporters   We advise you to leave the yards now. You
made a big hit, but that's all over now.   (*They leave*)
(*Shouting from rear, spreading toward front. The
WORKERS stand up*)

Workers   They're bringing the men from the central
office. (*The TWO WORKERS' LEADERS are brought
forward, handcuffed, by detectives*)

A Worker (*to the handcuffed LEADER*)   Take it easy,
William, not every day is dark.

Another (*shouts after the group*)   Bloody brutes!

Worker If they think this will hold things up they're off the
track. Our men have thought of everything.
*(In a vision JOAN sees herself as a criminal, beyond the
familiar world)*

Joan Why are the men who gave me the letter
    handcuffed? What
    is in the letter? I could do nothing
    that would have to be done by force and
    would provoke force. Someone like that would
    stand full of malice against his fellows
    past the reach of any settlement
    customary among mankind.
    Ceasing to belong, he could
    no longer find his way
    in a world now unfamiliar. Over his head
    the stars would move without
    the ancient rule. Words
    would change their meaning for him. Innocence
    would leave him, the pursuer and pursued.
    He can look at nothing without suspicion.
    I couldn't be like that. That's why I'm going.
    For three days Joan was seen
    in Packingtown, in the swamp of the stockyards
    descending from step to step
    to clear away the mud and manifest
    to the lowest. Three days striding
    downward, weakening on the third and
    swallowed by the swamp at last. Say:
    It was too cold. *(She gets up and goes.
    Snow is falling)*

Worker I knew from the first she'd beat it when the real
snow came. *(THREE WORKERS come by, look around
for someone, fail to find him, and go away.)*
(As darkness falls, a writing appears:)
    The snow begins to fall
    Will anyone stay at all?
    Here, as they always have, today
    Stony ground and the poor will stay.

PIERPONT MAULER CROSSES THE BORDER
OF POVERTY

Street corner in Chicago.
Mauler (*to one of the DETECTIVES*)
No further, let's turn back now, what do you say?
Admit it: you laughed. I said, Let's turn back now
and you laughed. They're shooting again.
Seems to be some resistance, eh? There's
something
I want to emphasize: don't give it
another thought if I turned back once or twice
as we approached the stockyards. Thinking
is nothing. I'm not paying you to think.
I may have my reasons. I'm known down there.
Now you're thinking again. It seems
I have blockheads with me. Anyway, let's turn
back.
I hope the woman I was looking for
has listened to the voice of sense down there
where all hell seems to have broken loose,
and left.
(*A NEWSBOY passes*)   Give me the papers! Let's see
how the livestock market's doing!
(*He reads, and turns deathly pale*)   Well, something's
happened here that changes things.
It says here in cold print that livestock's down
to 30 and not a head is being sold
because, it says here in cold print, the packers
are ruined and have left the livestock market.
It also says that Mauler and Slift, his friend, are
the worst hit of them all. That's what it says and
it means
that things have reached a point that certainly
wasn't striven for

but is greeted with relief. I can give them no
　　more help
having freely offered
all my livestock for the use of every man
and no man took it and therefore I am free
and beyond claims and hereby
I dismiss you, crossing
the border of poverty, for I no longer need you.
Henceforth no one will want to knock me down.

The Two Detectives   Then we may go.

Mauler   You may indeed, and so may I, wherever I want.
Even to the stockyards.
And as for the thing made of sweat and money
which we have erected in these cities:
now it looks as if a man
had made a building, the biggest in the world and
the costliest and most practical, but
by mistake and because it was cheap he used
　　dog-shit
for material, so that it would be pretty hard
to stay there and at last his only claim
to fame was that he had made the biggest stink
　　in the world.
Anyone who gets out of a building like that
should be a cheerful man.

A Detective (*departing*)   Well, that's the end of him.

Mauler   Bad luck lays low a man of low degree:
Me it must raise to spirituality.

*A deserted part of the stockyards. JOAN, running toward
the city, overhears TWO PASSING WORKERS.*

First Worker   First they let loose the rumor that work
would start up again, full blast, in the slaughterhouses.
Now that some of the workers have left the yards so as
to be on hand tomorrow morning, it's suddenly being
said that the slaughterhouses won't open at all, because
P. Mauler has ruined them.

Second Worker The Communists turned out to be right.
The masses shouldn't have broken ranks. The more so
as all the factories in Chicago would have called a
general strike tomorrow.

First Worker We weren't informed of that here.

Second Worker That's bad. Some of the messengers must
have failed us. A lot of people would have stayed if
they'd known that. In the teeth of the force the police
employed. (*Wandering around, JOAN hears voices*)

Voice The one who does not arrive
　　　　　knows no excuse. The stone does not
　　　　　excuse the man knocked down.
　　　　　Let not even the one who has arrived
　　　　　bore us with reports of difficulties
　　　　　but let him deliver silently
　　　　　himself or what has been confided to him.

(*JOAN has stood still at this. Now she runs in another
direction*)

Voice We gave you an assignment
　　　　　our position was pressing
　　　　　we didn't know who you were
　　　　　you might perform our assignment and you might
　　　　　also betray us.
　　　　　Did you perform it?

(*JOAN runs further and is halted by a new voice*)

Voice Where there is waiting, there must be arrival!
(*Looking around for rescue from the voices, JOAN hears
voices on all sides*)

Voices The net with one mesh torn
　　　　　has no more use.
　　　　　The fish swim through it at that point
　　　　　as if no net were there.
　　　　　All the meshes
　　　　　are suddenly useless.

(*JOAN falls to her knees*)

Joan O truth, shining light! Darkened by a snowstorm
　　　　in an evil hour!

Lost to sight from that moment! Oh, the force of
   snowstorms!
Oh, weakness of the flesh! What do you let live,
   hunger?
What outlasts you, frost of the night?
I must turn back! (*She runs back*)

X

PIERPONT MAULER HUMBLES HIMSELF
AND IS EXALTED

The Black Straw Hat Mission.

Martha (*to another BLACK STRAW HAT*)   Three days ago
a messenger from the meat king Pierpont Mauler came
to tell us that Pierpont Mauler himself wants to guarantee
our rent and also join us in a big campaign for the poor.

Mulberry   Mr. Snyder, it's Saturday night. I'm asking you
to pay your rent, which is very low, or get out of my
building.

Snyder   Mr. Mulberry, we're waiting now for Mr. Pierpont
Mauler, who has promised us his support.

Mulberry   Dick, Albert, will you kindly put the furniture in
the street?   (*Two men start carrying the furniture onto
the street*)

Black Straw Hats   Alas, they're taking the repentance
            bench!
      And now their greedy grasp
      threatens organ and pulpit.
      And louder we cry:
      If only rich Mr. Mauler
      would come to save us
      with his money!

Snyder   For seven days the masses have been standing
in the rusting stockyards, removed at last from
work.
Set free from any shelter, now they stand
under rain and snow.
Above them the zenith of an unknown decision.
Oh, Mr. Mulberry, my dear friend, hot soup now
and some music and they're ours. In my head
I see the Kingdom of Heaven all complete.
If we get a band and some decent soup, rich
for a change, God's worries will be over
and all of Bolshevism
will worry us no more.

Black Straw Hats   The dams of faith have burst
in our city of Chicago
and the muddy torrent of materialism
swirls in menace around the last of its houses.
Look, it's swaying, look, it's sinking!
Stick it out, though: rich man Mauler's coming!
He's on the way right now with all his money!

A Black Straw Hat   Where can we put the public now,
Major?   (*Three poor people enter, MAULER among them*)

Snyder (*yells at them*)   Soup, that's all they want! No soup
here! Just the word of God! We'll be rid of them at once
when they hear that.

Mauler   Here are three men coming to their God.

Snyder   Sit down over there and keep quiet.
(*The THREE sit down*)

A Man (*entering*)   Is Pierpont Mauler here?

Snyder   No, but we're expecting him.

Man   The packers want to talk to him and the
stockbreeders are yelling for him. (*He leaves*)

Mauler (*front*)   I hear they're looking for a Mauler.
I knew him: a blockhead. Now they're searching
high and low, in heaven and hell
for that Mauler who was dumber all his life
than a dirty drunken bum.

(rises and goes over to the BLACK STRAW HATS)
> I knew a man who once was asked
> for a hundred dollars. And he had about ten
>> million.
> And he came along without the hundred but threw
> the ten million away
> and gave himself.

(He takes TWO of the Black Straw Hats and kneels with them at the repentance bench)
> I wish to confess.
> No one, friends, who ever knelt here
> was as vile as I.

Black Straw Hats   Don't lose confidence
> be not of little faith!
> He's sure to come, he's already near
> with all his money.

A Black Straw Hat   Is he here yet?

Mauler   I beg you, sing a hymn! For in my heart
> there's lightness and heaviness at once

Two Musicians   One piece, no more.

(They intone a hymn. The BLACK STRAW HATS join in absently, looking at the door)

Snyder *(over account-books)*   I won't say how this comes
>> out.
>> Quiet!
Bring me the account-book and the unpaid bills. It's come
to that.

Mauler   I charge myself with exploitation
> abuse of power, expropriation of all
> in the name of property. For seven days I held
> this city Chicago by the throat
> until it croaked.

A Black Straw Hat   That's Mauler!

Mauler   Nevertheless I plead that on the seventh
> I stripped myself of everything, so that here
> I stand with no possessions.
> Not guiltless, but remorseful.

Snyder   Are you Mauler?

Mauler   Yes, and mangled by remorse.

Snyder (*crying out loud*)   And without money? (*to the BLACK STRAW HATS*)   Pack everything up, I hereby suspend all payments.

Musicians   If that's the man you've been expecting
to give you money to pay us with
we can go. Good night. (*They leave*)

Chorus of Black Straw Hats (*gazing after the departing MUSICIANS*)

We were awaiting with prayers
the wealthy Mauler, but in walked
the man converted.
His heart
he brought us, but not his money.
Therefore our hearts are moved, but
our faces are long.

(*The BLACK STRAW HATS sing their last hymns in garbled fashion as they sit on their last chairs and benches*)

Black Straw Hats   By the waters of Lake Michigan
we sit down and weep.
Take the proverbs off the walls
wrap the hymn-books in the cover of the
beaten flag
for we can pay our bills no more
and against us rise the snowstorms
of advancing winter.

(*Then once more they sing "Go into the thick of the fight." MAULER looks on with a BLACK STRAW HAT and joins in*)

Snyder   Quiet! Out now, everybody out, (*to MAULER*)
especially you!
Where's the rent for forty months from the
unconverted
whom Joan drove out? She drove *him* here
instead!
Joan, give me back my rent for forty months!

Mauler   I see you would have liked to build your house
within my shadow. For you a man
is what can help you, just as for me
only what was booty was a man.
But if only what is helped were called a man
there'd be no difference. Then you'd need
   drowning men.
For then it would be your business
to be straws. Thus everything abides
in the mighty orbit of merchandise, as of the stars.
This lesson, Snyder, would embitter many.
I see, however, that as I am now
I'm the wrong man for you.

(*As MAULER is about to leave, the MEAT KINGS meet
him at the door, all deathly pale*)

Packers   Exalted Mauler! We beg to be forgiven
for seeking you out, disturbing
the complex feelings in your giant head.
The fact is, we're ruined. Chaos is around us
and over us the zenith of an unknown intention.
What are your plans for us, Mauler?
What will your next steps be? We ask because
we felt the blows you rained upon our necks.

(*The STOCKBREEDERS enter in great commotion, also
deathly pale*)

Stockbreeders   Damn you, Mauler, is this where you slink
   off to?
Pay for our livestock instead of getting converted.
Your money, not your soul! You wouldn't need
to relieve your conscience in a place like this
if you hadn't relieved us of what was in our
   pockets.
Pay for our livestock!

Graham (*comes forward*)   Permit us, Mauler, to give you a
   brief account
of the battle that began this morning, lasted
for seven hours, and ended by plunging us
all into the abyss.

Mauler   Oh, everlasting slaughter! Nowadays
           things are no different from ancient times
           When men bloodied each other's heads with iron!

Graham   Remember, Mauler, that by contracts
           to deliver meat to you, you made us
           buy meat during these days, even if
           it was from you, for only you had meat.
           Well, when you went away at noon, Slift tightened
           his grip upon our throats. With stubborn cries
           he kept on driving prices up until
           they stood at 95. And then the ancient
           National Bank called a halt. Bleating, the kind
           old lady, full of responsibility, threw Canadian
              yearlings
           onto the shattered market and prices stood
              aquiver.
           But scarcely had Slift in his madness become
              aware
           of those few widely-travelled little steers than he
              grabbed them at 95
           the way a drunkard who's guzzled an oceanful
           and still feels thirsty greedily laps up
           one drop more. The beldame saw, and shuddered.
           Then indeed there sprang to her side, to support
              the old lady
           Loew and Levi, Wallox and Brigham, men of the
              highest reputation
           and mortaged themselves and all they owned,
              down to the last eraser
           as a promise to bring forth
           in three days from the Argentine and Canada
           the last remaining head of cattle—they even vowed
           to seize unborn ones, ruthlessly, anything oxlike
           calfly, hoggish! Slift yells: "Not three days from
              now!
           Today! Today!" and drives the price up. And in
              floods of tears

the banks threw themselves into the final battle.
They had to deliver the goods and therefore buy.
Sobbing, Levi himself dealt a body-blow
to one of Slift's brokers. Brigham tore his beard
    out
screaming: 96! At that point
an elephant that happened to get in
would have been squashed like a berry.
Office-boys, gripped by despair, bit one another
without a word, as steeds in olden times
would bite each other's flanks in the thick of the
    battling riders.
Unsalaried clerks, renowned for nonchalance
were heard gnashing their teeth that day.
And still we bought and bought: we had to buy.
Then Slift said: 100! You could have heard
a pin drop, that's how quiet it became.
And as quietly as that the banks collapsed
like trampled sponges, formerly hefty and firm
suspending payment now like breath. Softly spoke
Levi, the graybeard, and everyone heard him:
    "Now
our packing plants are yours, we can no longer
fulfill our contracts," and so, meat-packer
after meat-packer, they sullenly laid
the shut-down, useless packing plants
at your feet, yours and Slift's, and left the field
and the brokers and salesmen closed their
    portfolios.
And in that instant, with a groan, as of relief
since no contract now compelled its purchase
livestock sank into the bottomless pit.
Unto prices it was given
to fall from quotation to quotation
like water hurtling from cliff to cliff
deep down into infinity. They didn't stop before 30.
So, Mauler, your contract's no good to you now.

Instead of gripping us by the throat, you choked
us.

What's the use of gripping a dead man's throat?

Mauler   So, Slift, that was how you managed
the fight I left to you!

Slift   Tear my head off.

Mauler   What good's your head?
Give me your hat, it's worth a nickel!
What's to be done
with all that livestock nobody has to buy?

Stockbreeders   Without becoming flustered
we ask you, sir, to tell us
whether, when and with what
you plan to pay for the livestock which
is bought but not paid for.

Mauler   Immediately, with this hat and with this boot.
Here's my hat for ten million dollars, here's
one of my shoes for five. I need the other.
Will that take care of it?

Stockbreeders   Alas, when moons ago
we led by ropes the frisky calf
and clean young steers
carefully fed to the depot in far Missouri
the folks shouted after us
after us as the trains rolled away
after us in their voices broken by toil:
"Don't drink up the money, fellows," and
"Here's hoping the price of livestock will rise!"
What do we do now?
How can we go home?
What shall we tell them when
we show the empty ropes
and empty pockets?
Mauler, how can we journey home like that?

Man (*who was there before, enters*)   Is Mauler here? A
letter for him from New York.

Mauler   I was the Mauler letters like that were meant for.

(*opens it, reads aside*)   "Dear Pierpont, we recently wrote
you that you should buy meat. Today, however, we advise
you to reach an agreement with the stockbreeders and
limit the quantity of livestock, so that prices will rally. In
this event we shall gladly be at your service. More
tomorrow, dear Pierpont.—Your friends in New York." No,
no, that won't work.

Graham What won't work?

Mauler I have friends in New York who claim to know a
way out. It doesn't look like that to me. Judge for
yourselves. (*He gives them the letter*)

> How completely different
> everything seems now. Give up the hunt, my
>   friends.
> Your property is gone: you must understand, it's
>   lost.
> Not for the reason that we are blest no more with
>   earthly
> goods—as not everyone can be—but rather
> because we have no sense of higher things.
> That's why we're poor!

Meyers Who are these New York friends of yours?

Mauler Horgan and Blackwell. Sell . . .

Graham Would that be Wall Street?

Mauler The man within, so cruelly oppressed . . .

Packers and Stockbreeders Exalted Mauler, kindly bring
>   yourself
> to step down from your lofty meditations
> to us! Think of the chaos that would swamp
> everything, and now that you are needed
> take upon yourself
> again, Mauler, the yoke of responsibility!

Mauler I don't like to do it.
> And I dare not do it alone. My ears still echo
> with the grumbling in the stockyards and the
> crackle of machine-guns. It would only work
> if it were sanctioned in really grand style

and conceived as vitally appropriate
to the public good. On those terms
it might work.

(*to SNYDER*)   Are there many Bible shops like this?

Snyder   Yes.

Mauler   And how are they doing?

Snyder   Badly.

Mauler   Doing badly, but there are many.
If we promoted your Black Straw Hats
grandly in your work, would you then—
provided with soup and music and
suitable Bible quotations, even with shelter
in extreme cases—spread the word
for us that we're good people? Planning good
      things
in a bad time? For it's only
by extreme measures, which might seem harsh
      because
they affect some people, quite a few really
in short: most people, nearly everybody
that we can now preserve this system of buying
and selling which is, after all, our way of life
and also has its seamy side.

Snyder   For nearly everybody. I understand. We would.

Mauler (*to the PACKERS*)   I am merging your packing
      plants
into one trust and taking over
half the shares.

Packers   A great mind!

Mauler (*to the STOCKBREEDERS*)   Listen, good friends!
(*They whisper*)
The problem that has troubled us is lifting.
Misery and hunger, riot, violence
have one cause and that cause can now be seen:
there was too much meat. This year
the meat market was glutted and therefore

the price of livestock dropped to zero. Now
to uphold it we, packer and stockbreeder, have
    joined forces
to set some bounds to this unbridled breeding:
to limit livestock entering the market
and cut excess from what's on hand, that is
burn one-third of the total livestock.

All Simple solution!

Snyder (*saluting*) Wouldn't it be possible, if all that
    livestock
is so worthless that it can be burned
simply to give it to the multitude
standing out there, who'd have such good use for
    it?

Mauler (*smiles*) Snyder, my good friend, you haven't
    grasped the root of the matter. The multitude
    standing out there: THEY ARE THE BUYERS!
(*to the others*) You'd hardly believe it. (*All smile for a
long time*)
Vile they may seem, superfluous, sometimes
burdensome even, but it can't elude
profounder insight that THEY are the buyers!
Likewise, a thing very many won't understand, it's
    necessary
to lock one-third of the workers out, because
labor too has glutted our market and must
be limited.

All The only way out!

Mauler And wages lowered!

All Columbus' egg!

Mauler All this is being done so that
in a gloomy time of bloody confusion
dehumanized humanity
when disturbances seemed unending in our cities
(Chicago's excited again by the rumored threat of
    a general strike)

the brute strength of the dim-sighted people
may not smash its own tools and crush its
    bread-basket underfoot
and law and order may return. That's why we are
    willing
to facilitate with liberal contributions
the work by which you Black Straw Hats
    encourage order.
It's true that there ought to be people among you
    again
like that girl Joan, who inspires trust
by her mere appearance.

A Broker (*rushing in*)   Glad tidings! The threatened strike
has been suppressed. They've jailed the criminals who
impiously troubled law and order.

Slift   Breathe freely now! The market's getting well!
    At last we've overcome the evil spell.
    The difficult task has once again been done:
    our plan holds good and now the world's begun
    to go the way we like to see it run. (*organ*)

Mauler   And now open wide your gate
    unto the weary and heavy-laden and fill the pot
      with soup.
    Strike up the music and we ourselves shall be
    the first to take our seats upon your benches
    and be converted.

Snyder   Open the doors! (*The doors are opened wide*)

Black Straw Hats (*sing, looking at the doors*)
    Let the net be cast! They're bound to come!
    The house they're leaving right now is their last!
    God's sending cold on them!
    God's sending rain on them!
    So they're bound to come! Let the net be cast!
    Welcome! Welcome! Welcome!
    Welcome below in our home!

    Bolt everything tight so that none can get out!

They're on their way down to us all right!
If they've no work to do
if they're deaf and blind too
we'll let nobody out! So bolt everything tight.
Welcome! Welcome! Welcome!
Welcome below in our home!

Whatever may come, pull all of it in!
Hat and head and shoe and leg and scamp and
    scum!
Its hat has gone sky-high
so it's coming here to cry!
Drag all of it in, whatever may come!
Welcome below in our home!

Here we stand! Now they're coming down!
Look, their misery drives them like animals to our
    hand!
Behold, they must come down!
Behold, they're coming down!
There's no escape down here! That's where we
    stand!
Welcome! Welcome! Welcome!
Welcome below in our home!

*Stockyards. Area in front of the Graham plant. The yards
are nearly empty. Only a few groups of WORKERS are
passing by.*
Joan (*comes up and asks*)   Did three people go by here
and ask for a letter?
(*Shouting from rear, spreading toward front. Then FIVE
MEN enter, escorted by SOLDIERS: the two from the
central office and the three from the power stations. ONE
of the men from the central office stops suddenly and
speaks to the SOLDIERS*)
Man   Now that you're taking us to jail, you should know
that we did what we did because we're on your side.

Soldier Keep moving, if you're on our side.

Man Wait a little!

Soldier Are you scared?

Man Yes, that too, but that's not what I mean. I only want
   you men to stop a while so I can tell you why you
   arrested us, because you don't know.

Soldiers (*laugh*) All right, tell us why we arrested you.

Man Without property yourselves, you help men of
   property because you don't yet see any possibility of
   helping men without property.

Soldier Is that so? Let's move on.

Man Wait! The sentence isn't finished.—but people with
   jobs are starting to help the jobless in this town. So the
   possibility is coming closer. Think of that.

Soldier I guess you want us to let you go.

Man Didn't you understand me? I only want you men to
   know that your time, too, is coming soon.

Soldiers Can we move on now?

Man Yes, we can move on now. (*They move on*)
   (*JOAN stands still and watches the arrested men go. Then
   she hears TWO PEOPLE beside her talking*)

One Man What sort of people are those?

Other Man Not one of them
        thought only of himself.
        No, they ran without rest
        to get bread for strangers.

One Why without rest?

Other The unjust man may cross the street in the open,
        but the just man hides.

One What becomes of them?

Other Although they
        work for low pay and are useful to many
        not one lives out his natural life
        eats his bread, dies satisfied and is
        buried with honors. No, they end
        before their time and are
        struck down and crushed and covered with earth
          in shame.

One Why do we never hear about them?
Other If you read in the papers that several criminals have
           been shot or
        thrown into the prisons, they're the ones.
One Will it always be that way?
Other No.
    (*As JOAN turns to go, she is hailed by the REPORTERS*)
Reporters Isn't this Our Lady of the Stockyards? Hello
there! Things went wrong! The general strike was called
off. The slaughterhouses are reopening, but only for
two-thirds of the work force and only at two-thirds pay.
But meat is getting dearer.
Joan Have the workers consented?
Reporters Sure. Only some of them knew a general strike
was planned, and they were forcibly expelled by the
police. (*JOAN falls down*)

XI

DEATH AND CANONIZATION
OF SAINT JOAN OF THE STOCKYARDS

*Now the house of the BLACK STRAW HATS is richly
furnished and decorated. Grouped in tiers, the BLACK
STRAW HATS with new flags, the PACKERS, the
STOCKBREEDERS and the WHOLESALERS stand
waiting for the GLOOMBS and LUCKERNIDDLES. The
doors are open.*

Snyder So our task finds happy ending
        God's footing has been found again
        For the highest good contending
        we have faced the depths of pain.
        Both our climbing and descending
        show what we can mean to you:

Now at last a happy ending
Now at last we've broken through!
(*A mass of POOR PEOPLE enter, with JOAN, supported by two POLICEMEN, at their head*)

Policemen Here is a homeless woman
we picked up in the stockyards
in a diseased condition. Her
last permanent residence was
allegedly here.

(*JOAN holds up the letter, as if she still wanted to deliver it*)

Joan Never will the man who has perished
take my letter from me.
Small service in a good cause, a service
to which I was bidden all my life, the only one!
I did not carry out.

(*While the POOR PEOPLE take seats on the benches to get their soup, SLIFT consults with the PACKERS and SNYDER*)

Slift That's our Joan, like an answer to our prayers. Let's cover her with glory. By her philanthropic activity in the stockyards, her spokesmanship of the poor, even by her speeches against us she helped us over some difficult weeks. She shall be our Saint Joan of the Stockyards. We will set her up as a saint and deny her no respect. On the contrary, her revelation here will serve as proof that we hold humaneness in high regard.

Mauler May the pure and childlike soul
not be absent from our roll
May her singing clear and free
sound amid our chorus too
All that imperils us may she
damn, speaking for us and you.

Snyder Rise, Joan of the stockyards
spokeswoman of the poor
comforter of the lowest depths!

Joan What a wind in the depths! What are the shouts

thou, snow, art silencing?
Eat your soup, you!
Don't spill the last bit of warmth, you
good-for-nothings! Eat your soup!
If only I had lived
as calmly as a cow
and yet delivered the letter I was given!

Black Straw Hats (*closing in on her*)
Sudden daylight makes her ache
after nights of stupefaction!
Only human was your action!
Only human your mistake!

Joan (*as the GIRLS reclothe her in the Black Straw Hat uniform*)
The noise of the factories has started again, you
can hear it.
Another chance to stop it
has been wasted.
The world resumes
its ancient course unaltered.
When it was possible to change it
I did not come; when it was necessary
for me, little person, to help
I stayed away.

Mauler Woe, that man cannot abide
in his stress the earthly bond
and that in his haughty stride
from the daily grind
that breaks his mind
toward an unknown
infinite throne
he hurtles far, above, beyond!

Joan Speeches I made in every market-place
and dreams were past counting but
I did injury to the injured
was useful to the injurers.

Black Straw Hats Alas, all stretching forth of might

achieves but patchwork lacking soul
if matter make not spirit whole.

Packers   And ever 'tis a glorious sight
when soul and business unite!

Joan   I've learned one thing and I know it on your
behalf, dying myself:
how can it be that there is something in you
that won't come out! WHAT do you know in your
knowing
that has no results?
I, for example, have done nothing.
Let nothing be counted good, although, as always,
it may seem
really helpful, and nothing henceforth be
considered honorable
except what changes this world once for all: it
needs it.
Like an answer to their prayers I came to the
oppressors!
Oh, goodness without results! Unnoticed attitude!
I have altered nothing.
Swiftly, fruitlessly vanishing from this world
I say unto you:
Take care that when you leave the world
you were not only good but are leaving
a good world!

Graham   We must take care to let her speeches pass only
when they're sensible. We shouldn't forget that she's been
in the stockyards.

Joan   You see, there's a gulf between top and bottom,
bigger
than between Mount Himalaya and the sea
and what goes on above
is not found out below
or what goes on below, above
and there are two languages, top and bottom
and two standards to measure by

and that which wears a human face
knows itself no more.

Packers and Stockbreeders (*very loud, so as to drown
   JOAN out*)

Top and bottom must apply
if the building's to be high.
That's why everyone must stay
in the place where they belong.
Day after day
man must do what fits his stature
for if he forgets his nature
all our harmonies go wrong.
Underdogs have weight below
The right man's right when up you go.
Woe to the man who'd rouse that host—
indispensable but
demanding, not
to be done without
and aware of that—
elements of the nethermost!

Joan   But those who are below are kept below
so that those above may stay above
and the vileness of those above is measureless
and even if they get better that would be
no help, because the system
they have built is peerless:
exploitation and disorder, beastly and therefore
past understanding.

Black Straw Hats (*to JOAN*)   Be a good girl! Hold your
          tongue!

Packers   Those who float in boundless spaces
cannot rise to higher places.
If you'd climb, you need a rung
and to reach for things aloft
you must make a downward tread.

Mauler   Action, alas, may break a head!

Black Straw Hats   Knowing your shoe is stained with gore

Packers do not try to pull it off!
You will need it more and more.

Black Straw Hats Keep conduct high and spirit young.
But do not forget to rue it!

Packers Do anything!

Black Straw Hats But always do it
with pangs of guilt, because
to be wise yourself
you despise yourself
and conscience has its claws!
Merchants, be spry!
When deals are forming
open or sly
you can't afford
to forget the splendid
word of the Lord
self-transforming
never ended.

Joan So anyone down here who says there is a God
although there's none to be seen
and He can be invisible and help them all the
same
should have his head banged on the pavement
until he croaks.

Slift Listen, you've got to say something to shut that girl
up. You must speak—anything at all, but loud!

Snyder Joan Dark, 25 years old, laid low by pneumonia in
the stockyards of Chicago, in the service of God, a fighter
and a sacrifice!

Joan And as for the ones that tell them they may be raised
in spirit
and still be stuck in the mud, they too should be
tossed out
heads down. It's not like that!
Only force helps where force rules, and
only men help where men are.

*(All sing the first verse of the chorale, to keep JOAN's
speeches from being heard)*

All   Fill the full man's plate! Hosanna!
          Greatness to the great! Hosanna!
          To him that hath shall be given! Hosanna!
          Give him city and state! Hosanna!
          To the victor a sign from heaven! Hosanna!
*During these declamations loudspeakers begin to
announce terrible news: POUND FALLS! BANK OF
ENGLAND CLOSES FOR FIRST TIME IN THREE
HUNDRED YEARS! and EIGHT MILLION UNEMPLOYED
IN U.S.A.! and FIVE-YEAR PLAN SUCCEEDS! and BRAZIL
POURS ONE YEAR'S COFFEE CROP INTO OCEAN! and
SIX MILLION UNEMPLOYED IN GERMANY! and THREE
THOUSAND BANKS FAIL IN U.S.A.! and STOCK
EXCHANGES AND BANKS CLOSED BY GOVERNMENT
ORDER IN GERMANY! and BATTLE BETWEEN POLICE
AND UNEMPLOYED OUTSIDE HENRY FORD'S PLANT IN
DETROIT! and BIGGEST EUROPEAN TRUST, MATCH
TRUST, GOES BANKRUPT! and FIVE-YEAR PLAN IN
FOUR YEARS!*
*Impressed by the terrible news, those not previously
engaged in declamation shout abuse at one another, such
as* "Filthy hog-butchers, you shouldn't have slaughtered
all that livestock!" *and* "Rotten stockbreeders, you should
have bred more livestock!" *and* "You crazy
money-grubbers, you should have hired more people
and paid more wages! Now who's going to eat our meat?"
and "Middlemen make meat expensive!" *and* "It's the
grain racket that makes livestock expensive!" *and*
"Railroad freight rates are choking us!" *and* "Bank
interest rates are ruining us!" *and* "Who can pay those
rents for barns and silos?" *and* "Why don't you start
plowing under?" *and* "We did plow under, but you aren't
plowing under!" *and* "The fault is yours and yours alone!"
and "Things won't get better until you're hanged!" *and*
"You should have been jailed long ago!" *and* "How come
you're still at large?"
*(All sing the second and third verse of the chorale. JOAN
is now inaudible)*

All   Pity the well-to-do! Hosanna!
Set them in Thy path! Hosanna!
Vouchsafe Thy grace, Hosanna!
and Thy help to him that hath! Hosanna!
Have mercy on the few! Hosanna!

(*Joan's talk is noticeably stopping*)

Help Thy class, which in turn helps Thee,
Hosanna!
with a liberal hand! Hosanna!
Stamp out hatred now! Hosanna!
Laugh with him who laughs! Allow, Hosanna!
his crimes a happy end! Hosanna!

(*During this verse the GIRLS have been trying to pour some soup down Joan's throat. Twice she has pushed the plate back. The third time she grabs it, holds it up and pours the contents out. Then she falls back and is now lying in the girls' arms, mortally wounded, giving no sign of life. SNYDER and MAULER step towards her*)

Mauler   Give her the flag!

(*The flag is presented to her. The flag drops from her hands*)

Snyder   Joan Dark, 25 years old, dead of pneumonia in the stockyards, in the service of God, a fighter and a sacrifice.

Mauler   Ah, what's pure
and has no flaw—
uncorrupted, helpful, whole—
moves us common folk to awe!
Rouses in our breast a newer
better soul!

(*All stand in speechless emotion for a long time. At a sign from SNYDER all the flags are gently lowered on JOAN until she is entirely covered by them. A rosy glow lights up the scene*)

Packers and Stockbreeders

Behold! Our human nature owns
immemorial desires

       by which toward the higher zones
       our spirit constantly aspires.
       We see the stars upon their thrones
       we sense a thousand ways to heaven
       yet downward by the flesh are driven
       and so in shame our pride expires.

Mauler A twofold power cuts and tears
       my miserable inner state
       like a jagged, deep-thrust knife:
       I'm drawn to what is truly great
       free from self and the profit rate
       and yet impelled to business life
       all unawares!

All Humanity! Two souls abide
       within thy breast!
       Do not put either one aside
       for life with both is best.
       Be two in one! Be here and there!
       Keep the lofty and the low one
       Keep the righteous and the raw one
       Keep the pair!